Introduction to

Time Series Analysis

Anusha Illukkumbura

MSc. Business Statistics
B.A. Social Statistics

Acknowledgement

First Edition
Copyright © (2021) by Anusha Illukkumbura
First Edition: November 2021
ISBN: 9798769616464

Find the data sets for given examples in excel sheet at https://www.facebook.com/groups/590090104970492/files or my website http://www.anushabooks.com/product/introduction-to-time-series-analysis/

BookAuthority Recognition
Introduction to Regression Analysis got rated as "Best Statistics EBooks for beginners" and one of the "Best Statistics EBooks all the time" by BookAuthority.org in 2021
Probability: Questions and Answers got rated as "Best New Statistics EBooks" and one of the "Best Statistics EBooks all the time" by BookAuthority.org in 2021

Preface

Introduction to Time Series Data Analysis is the sixth book in Easy Statistics Series. Aim of the Easy Statistics Series is to simplify the complicated topics in Statistics.

Many advanced books on time series data analysis are too complicated and exhausting for the students. But this book gives simple and quick explanation about complicated topics on time series data analysis.

This book covers topics and examples on
- Time Series Patterns
- Decomposition models
- Data Smoothing Methods
- Stationary time series
- Advanced Concepts used in Time Series Data Analysis
- Residual Tests
- AR , MA and ARIMA models
- ARCH/GARCH Models
- Vector Auto-regressive Models
- Vector Error Correction Models
- ARDL model

The examples are solved using manual calculations and E-views statistical software. This book can be used as a self-study material and a text book. It is suggested to have a prior knowledge on Regression Analysis before learning Time Series Analysis. Easy Statistics Series have a book on Regression Analysis as well. You can get a wide knowledge on Regression Analysis after reading "Introduction to Regression Analysis" written by me.

Any suggestions to further improve the contents of this edition would be warmly appreciated. For any further suggestions, please contact me at website : www.anushabooks.com
email : anusha.illukkumbura@yahoo.com

Anusha Illukkumbura©
MSc. Business Statistics (University of Moratuwa, Sri Lanka)
B.A. Social Statistics (University of Kelaniya, Sri Lanka)
November 2021

Table of Content

Chapter One : Time Series Data... 1

    1.1   What is a Time Series?... 1

    1.2   Time Series Components.. 2

    1.3   Time Series Model Accuracy Measures 4

        1.3.1   MAD/MAE... 4

        1.3.2   BIAS 5

        1.3.3   MSE /MSD 5

        1.3.4   MAPE 6

    1.4   Linear Line Estimation Methods 6

        1.4.1   Free Hand Method 6

        1.4.2   Semi Average Method 7

        1.4.3   Least Square Method 8

        1.4.4   Moving Average 9

    1.5   Seasonal Patterns Estimation Methods. 14

    1.6   Basic Time Series Forecasting Methods 15

        1.6.1   Naïve Method 15

        1.6.2   Linear Trend Forecast.................................... 15

        1.6.3   Non Linear Forecast 15

    1.7   Cyclic Pattern Estimation....................................... 15

        1.7.1   Weighted moving average............................. 15

Chapter Two: Stationary Time Series 21

    2.1   What is a stationary time series? 21

    2.2   How to make a stationary Time Series Model........ 22

        2.2.1   Decomposition Techniques............................ 22

        2.2.2   Smoothing Methods 23

        2.2.3   Differencing.. 27

        2.2.4   Transforming to log 28

Chapter Three: Serial Correlation.. 29

3.1   Autocorrelation/ Serial Correlation.. 29

3.2   ACF and PACF 32

3.3   Tests for Serial Correlation 36

3.4   Heteroskedasticity.. 39

3.5   Volatility.. 43

3.6   Unit Root Test... 44

3.7   Random Walk.. 44

Chapter Four: ARIMA 46

4.1   AR 46

4.2   MA 47

4.3   Backshift Operator... 50

4.4   Invertibility... 51

4.5   ARMA model... 70

4.6   ARIMA Model 71

4.7   Seasonal ARIMA Modeling... 71

Chapter Five: ARCH/GARCH..100

5.1   Introduction 100

5.2   Parsimonious Models 101

5.3   ARCH Model..102

Chapter Six..122

Vector Auto-Regression Model and 122

Vector Error Correction Model...122

6.1   Vector Auto Regression Model..122

6.2   Error Correction Model..123

6.3   Granger causality..124

6.4   Short Run and Long Run causality....................................144

6.5   Impulse Responses 146

6.6   Vector Error Correction Model Estimation......................148

Chapter Seven: 163

Autoregressive Distributed Lag Model (ARDL) 163

    7.1   Introduction 163

    7.2   ARDL bound test.. 163

    7.3   Error Correction Model...................................... 164

    7.4   CUSUM Test 165

Example 1.1: Semi Average Method 7

Example 1.2 : Least Square Method.. 8

Example 1.3 : Simple Moving Average... 10

Example 1.4 : MA order 2/3/4 11

Example 1.5 : BIAS, MAD, MSE, MAPE 16

Example 2.1 : Simple exponential smoothing............................... 25

Example 2.2 : Double Moving Average 27

Example 3.1: Autocorrelation 30

Example 3.2: Autocorrelation 31

Example 4.1: Backshift Operator 51

Example 4.2 : Invetibility 53

Example 4.3 : MA(1) Model 55

Example 4.4: AR(1) 64

Example 4.5: ARIMA (PDQ) 72

Example 4.6 : ARIMA 81

Example 4.7: Seasonal ARIMA 88

Example 5.1: ARCH/GARCH model for ASPI data 103

Example 6.1 : VAR Model 125

Example 6.2 : VECM 148

Example 7.1 :ARDL Model 167

Chapter One : Time Series Data

1.1 What is a Time Series?

Time series is a collection of observations taken at equal time interval. A time series is a collection of observations or data obtained for a specific variable during a specific, defined and sequence time intervals. In a time series model, observations of a variable are recorded against equal time intervals.

In statistics two types of models are used to analyze data series. They are causal models and time series models. (Regression analysis falls under the category of causal models. In regression analysis, variables are identified as independent and dependent variables.)

If the observations of time periods of $t_1, t_2 \ldots t_n$ are identified as $Y_1, Y_2 \ldots Y_n$, then $Y_1, Y_2 \ldots Y_n$ is called a time series. $t_1, t_2 \ldots t_n$ are equal time periods. $Y_1, Y_2 \ldots Y_n$ are observations. $Y_1, Y_2 \ldots Y_n$ is also called an **array** of time series. Array of time series can be represented by Y_t (Y_t, where t=1,2...n).

The function of the relationship between time (t) and the observations of the variable (Y) is Y=f(t).

When the time series is lengthy, then the time series analysis is more accurate. But there is short term, medium and long term forecasting methods in time series data analysis. Applying the suitable time series method for the data set increases the accuracy of the analysis.

Uses of Time Series Models

Time series models are useful in studying the past behavior of the variables. It can be used to predict /estimate/forecast the behavior of variables related to business or economy. The time series models can be used to formulate policy decision and future planning. They also can be used to identify interdependencies of two or more time series. Time series data analysis is important to identify underlying forces and structures in a time series variable and to identify a suitable model for forecasting purpose. Future value of a time series can be predicted using present and past observations. The adjacent observations of a time series are dependent. As an example, think about inflation rate of a country, last year's inflation rate has an influence on this year's inflation rate and this year's on next year.

There are monthly, hourly and daily time series. Body temperature taken from a patient hourly is a time series. Daily rain fall, monthly sales of a company can also be analyzed using time series data analysis methods. Time series data analysis can be used to analyze economic data and business data. We can do predictions using a single time series or several time series. As an example time series data of inflation rate can be used to predict coming trends of inflation rate of a country. Both inflation rate and unemployment rate can be used to understand the interdependencies of these two variables chronologically.

Three steps of fitting a time series model

1. Model Identification
2. Model Estimation
3. Model Validation

First, in model identification step, the data should be graphed and we should identify the patterns in data. Then we can calculate descriptive statistics of the data variable, such as mean, standard deviation, percentiles and autocorrelation. We should identify outliers as well. This first step will help us to identify trend or seasonal patterns of the data set.

Then in model estimation method we try to fit a suitable forecasting model for the dataset. Here we estimate parameters and do residual tests to confirm if the models are correct. After that model validation step consists of identifying how the estimated model performs in case of intended application.

1.2   Time Series Components

It is assumed that fluctuations of a time series are due to coinciding four types of variations. They are

1. Long Term Trend

2. Seasonal variation
3. Cyclical variation
4. Irregular variations

Above four are called components of a time series. Components of time series are used to describe the variation of a time series. Some argues irregular variations are not a component.

Trend shows a long term increment or decrement of data series.
Seasonal variation show similar repetitive patterns during similar (equivalent) and sequential time periods. In seasonal patterns data series is influenced by seasonally fluctuated data. Seasonal temperature of a country during few years shows seasonal patterns. Cyclic patterns are the alternative upward and downward movements in a time series plot. This can also be identified as recurring sequences of points above and below the trend line lasting at least over one year.

Irregular pattern is a time series with random effect. These types of patterns can happen due to unexpected shocks/influenced/reasons. They can also be identified as residuals or deviations from actual time series. Outliers also fall into this category.

As an example, Sri Lanka had a long term increasing number of foreign tourists, but in 2019 ISIS attacked few tourists' destinations in Sri Lanka, which caused sudden fall of foreign tourists who are visiting Sri Lanka. This can be identified as an external shock which make the data series irregular.

There are two approaches to describe the relationship among the above components. They are **additive** models and **multiplicative** models. These models will be discussed under decomposition methods in this book.

Figure 1.1: Time Series Pattern

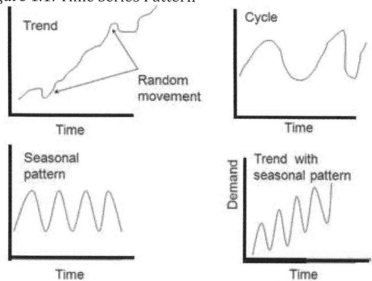

1.3 Time Series Model Accuracy Measures

Accuracy measures are used to measure forecast accuracy of a model or to forecast error. Error is the difference between forecasted value and actual value.

There are four basic methods to evaluate the variability of time series models. These methods measure the accuracy of the model. The smaller values of these accuracy measures represent better model. They are

1. MAD
2. BIAS
3. MSE
4. MAPE

1.3.1 MAD/MAE

Mean Absolute Deviation is a technique to measure the variability of a dataset. This is also called Mean Absolute Error (MAE). It is the average distance between each data point and the mean. Simply ,

Mean Absolute Deviation is the average of the sum of the absolute error.

How to calculate MAD
1. Calculate the mean
2. Calculate the absolute deviation
3. Calculate the average of the absolute deviations

$$MAD = \frac{\sum |Y - \hat{Y}|}{n}$$

1.3.2 BIAS

BIAS value is the average value of the difference between the estimator's expected value and true value of the parameter. This is simple called the average error. The difference between the estimator's expected value and true value of the parameter is the error term. This also measures the variability of a new estimated time series model.

How to calculate BIAS
1. Calculate the error term
2. Calculate the average of the error term

$$BIAS = \frac{\sum Y - \hat{Y}}{n}$$

1.3.3 MSE /MSD

Mean Square Error (MSE) is the average of the square of the difference between actual and estimated values. (Difference between actual and estimated values is the error term).

How to calculate MSE
1. Calculate the error term
2. Square the error term
3. Calculate the average of the squared error term

$$MSE = \frac{\sum (Y - \hat{Y})^2}{n}$$

The squaring is necessary to remove any negative signs. It also gives more weight to larger differences. This is also called the Mean Squared Deviation (MSD) Error. When square root of MSE is taken it becomes Root Mean Squared Error (RMSE) which is a helpful key performance indicator (KPI) of time series models.

1.3.4 MAPE

Mean Absolute Percentage Error (MAPE) is the average of the absolute value of the percentage error of the forecasted model.

Percentage error is the sum of "the each percentage of the difference between actual value and forecasted value divided by actual value"

How to calculate MAPE

1. Calculate the absolute percentage error

$$\frac{|Y - \hat{Y}|}{Y}$$

2. Sum up the absolute percentage error

$$\sum \frac{|Y - \hat{Y}|}{Y}$$

3. Find the average of the Absolute Percentage Error (MAPE)

$$\frac{\sum \frac{|Y - \hat{Y}|}{Y}}{n}$$

This measure is easy to understand as it provides the error in percentages. We will be calculating above measures at the end of the chapter.

1.4 Linear Line Estimation Methods

There are few methods to calculate straight line to a time series. They are

1. Free hand method
2. Semi Average Method
3. Least Square method
4. Moving Averages method

1.4.1 Free Hand Method

In free hand method first data is marked in a scatter plot, and then using mind estimation we can draw a line which can represent all the points. This line can be identified as a trend line. This method is person biased; therefore it is not useful in decision making and formal data analysis.

1.4.2 Semi Average Method

In semi average method, we try to find the trend using two points. These two points are calculated by taking the average of the data set which is divided into two.

If the data set has an even number of observations then the data set can equally divided into two parts. If there are odd numbers of observations then first we remove the middle number and then divide the data set into two. Now let's see how to calculate semi moving average method.

Example 1.1: Semi Average Method

Below is the quarterly sale income of a grocery store from 1990 to 1993.

Time	1990	1991	1992	1993	1994	1995	1996	1997
Sales	7500	6000	5400	6800	8600	6500	6300	8000

Time	1998	1999	2000	2001	2002	2003	2004	2005
Sales	9000	7000	6600	8500	10000	7800	7200	9500

Now above data can be divided into two groups. First group is from 1990 to 1997. Second group is from 1998 to 2005.
Average of the first group of data
= (7500+6000+5400+6800+8600+6500+6300+8000)/8
=55100/8 =6880
Average of the second group of data
= (9000+7000+6600+8500+10000+7800+7200+9500)/8
=65600/8 =8200
Scatter plot in figure 1.2 shows estimated line drawn using Semi Average Method.

Figure 1.2 : Scatterplot

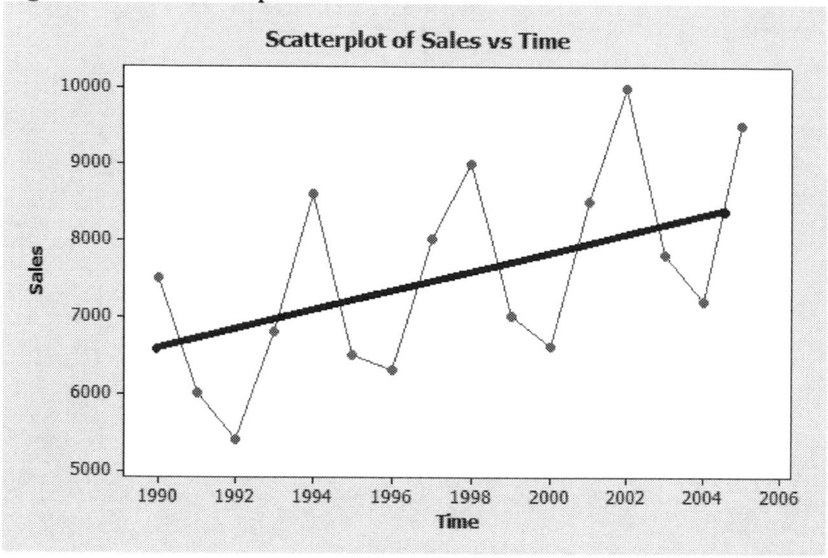

Scatterplot of Sales vs Time

1.4.3   Least Square Method

Least square method is widely used in regression analysis. We use this method to fit a suitable line to the time series data. Below is an example of how to calculate an estimated forecasting line using least square method.

Example 1.2 : Least Square Method

Below are details of a shoe company on its advertising cost and sales for 5 years. All values are in thousand dollars.

year	2010	2011	2012	2013	2014
x	7	9	11	13	15
y	102	127	122	132	152

I. Find the regression model

II. Check for the significance of the parameters at 5% of significance level.

Answer

I)   Calculate statistics given in below table

Table 1.1: Descriptive Statistics

Year	x	y	x^2	y^2	xy
2010	7	102	49	10404	714
2011	9	127	81	16129	1143
2012	11	122	121	14884	1342
2013	13	132	169	17424	1716
2014	15	152	225	23104	2280
Total	**55**	**635**	**645**	**81945**	**7195**

$\bar{x}$= 11 $\bar{y}$= 127

$$b_1 = \frac{n\Sigma xy - \Sigma x \Sigma y}{n\Sigma x^2 - (\Sigma x)^2}$$

$$b_1 = \frac{5 * 7195 - 55 * 635}{5 * 645 - 55 * 55}$$

$$b_1 = 5.25$$

$$b_0 = \bar{y} - b_1 \bar{x}$$

$$b_0 = 127 - 5.25 * 11$$

$$b_0 = 69.3$$

Regression model is Y = 69.3 + 5.25 x

Refer "Introduction to Regression Analysis" in Easy Statistics Series for more understanding on ordinary least square method and regression analysis.

1.4.4 Moving Average

Moving average method removes short term patterns from a time series. It is a time series smoothing method. Moving average method is better for removing short term patterns.

Moving average is calculated by taking the average for set of observations inside a time series. For a time series with odd numbers of observations Moving average can be calculated by taking the average of 3,5,7 nearby observations. When the numbers of observations are even, then use moving average for time intervals of 2 or 4. When less observations are taken to count the average, then the line become smoother. That means when a moving average is calculate for time periods of 3 , that line is smoother than a line which is calculated for time periods of 5. These time intervals are called length of moving average. The length can be 2,3,4,5 or more. But the fitted line is smoother when the length is smaller.

Moving Average method is better than free hand method and semi average method. But when there are outliers or unusual values, this method is not efficient. If there are outliers then it will results unusual curves in the estimated line. Another disadvantage of this method is lacking observations at the first and last places in the newly created array. Now let's do a sample on simple moving average.

Example 1.3 : Simple Moving Average
Find the moving average model for the below data series.

Year	1981	1982	1983	1984	1985	1986	1987	1988	1989	1990
Number	1.45	1.55	1.61	1.6	1.74	1.92	1.95	2.04	2.06	1.8
Year	1991	1992	1993	1994	1995	1996	1997	1998	1999	2000
Number	1.73	1.77	1.9	1.82	1.65	1.73	1.88	2	2.08	1.88

Answer
Below answer is calculated for 3 years length

Year	Number	MA		Year	Number	MA
1981	1.45			1991	1.73	1.97
1982	1.55			1992	1.77	1.86
1983	1.61			1993	1.9	1.77
1984	1.6	1.54		1994	1.82	1.8
1985	1.74	1.59		1995	1.65	1.83
1986	1.92	1.65		1996	1.73	1.79
1987	1.95	1.75		1997	1.88	1.73
1988	2.04	1.87		1998	2	1.75
1989	2.06	1.97		1999	2.08	1.87
1990	1.8	2.02		2000	1.88	1.99

Moving average for three periods is calculated by taking the average for each 3 years length

$$MA_{1984} = \frac{1.45+1.55+1.61}{3} = 1.54$$

$$MA_{1985} = \frac{1.55+1.61+1.60}{3} = 1.59$$
$$MA_{1986} = \frac{1.61+1.60+1.74}{3} = 1.65$$

Likewise take the average of every three observations of the data series to obtain the moving average estimations.

Now let's compare the fitted line (moving average line) and actual data series in a scatter plot. See figure 1.3.

Figure 1.3 : Moving Average

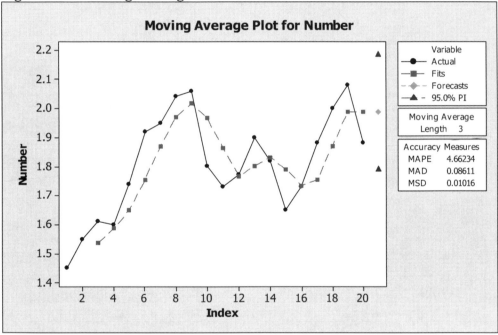

When the length of the moving average is less , then the fitted line become more reliable.

Example 1.4 : MA order 2/3/4

Find the moving average model order 3 and moving average model order 5 for the below data series.

Year	1981	1982	1983	1984	1985	1986	1987	1988	1989	1990
Number	1.45	1.55	1.61	1.6	1.74	1.92	1.95	2.04	2.06	1.8
Year	1991	1992	1993	1994	1995	1996	1997	1998	1999	2000
Number	1.73	1.77	1.9	1.82	1.65	1.73	1.88	2	2.08	1.88

11

We can use statistics software to calculate moving average and model the lines.

Below figure show the data series model for the scatter plot.
MINITAB : Graph > Scatter plot

Figure 1.4: Scatter Plot of observations

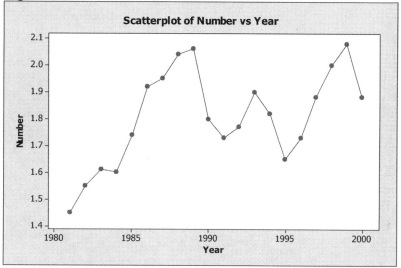

Now let's compare original data series and the fitted models which are calculated according to different moving average lengths.

Minitab: Stat > Time Series > Moving Average> MA length 3 > select center the moving average > select generate forecast , number of forecast :1

Figure 1.5 :Moving Average Length 3

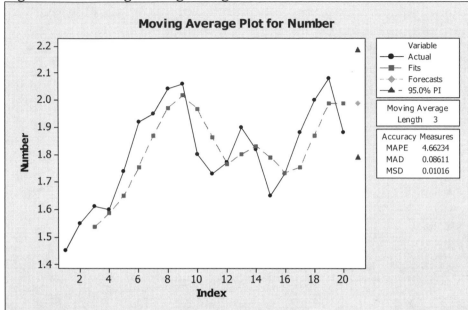

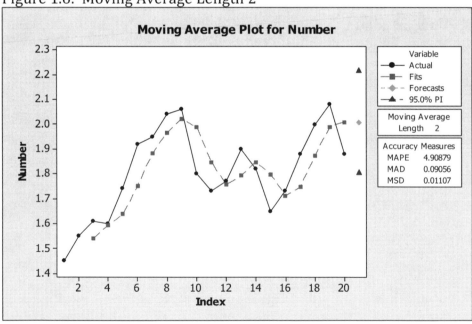

Figure 1.7: Moving Average Length 4

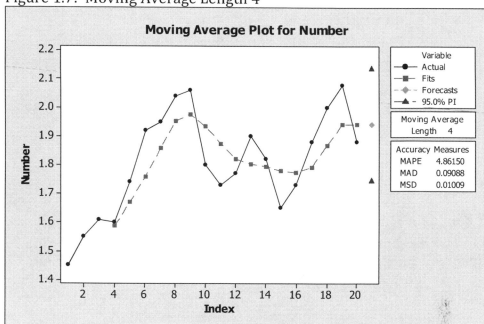

Below table shows the accuracy measures of different MA lengths. MA length 3 shows the less accuracy values. Therefore for the above dataset MA order 3 is more suitable for predictions.

Moving Order	MAPE	MAD	MSD
2	4.90879	0.09056	0.01107
3	4.66234	0.08611	0.01016
4	4.8615	0.09088	0.01009

1.5   Seasonal Patterns Estimation Methods.

There are three types of seasonal pattern estimation
1. Method of simple averages
    Data of each month or quarter is expressed as a percentage of the average of the year
    Seasonal Index = seasonal average/ General average

2. Ratio to trend method

Seasonal variation is a fraction of trend
Find the yearly averages / totals for all the years
Fit a trend
Obtain monthly/quarterly trend values by adjusting equation

3. Ratio to moving average method
   Original value in the time series expressed as a % of moving average
   $$\frac{T*C*S*I}{T*C}*100$$

1.6 Basic Time Series Forecasting Methods

1.6.1 Naïve Method
In naïve forecasting method we use the last period's actual observation as the current period's forecast value. Therefore for the time period of t, the forecasted value is the observed value of the time period (t-1).
$y_t = y_{t-1}$

1.6.2 Linear Trend Forecast
Linear trend forecast method is used to estimate the linear relationship using least square method. Between time and the responsive variable. Linear trend takes the form of equation
$y_t = a+bx$
a and b are constants and x is the time series variable. y_t is the estimated value.

1.6.3 Non Linear Forecast
In non linear forecast method, non linear relationship between time and responsive variable is calculated using least square method. Non-linear trend takes the form of equation
$y_t = a+bx+ cx^2$

1.7 Cyclic Pattern Estimation

1.7.1 Weighted moving average.
Weighted moving average assign heavier weight to more recent data points. In simple moving average estimate, the weights are equally distributed. In weight moving average the weight decrease by equal amount but in exponential moving average, the rate of decrease between one weight and its previous weight is exponential.

Example 1.5 : BIAS, MAD, MSE, MAPE

Given below are the sales of a company for 12 months. Now let's try to fit a suitable time series model for the data set. After that we should calculate the model accuracy measures to understand which model is the most suitable model for forecasting.

Period	1	2	3	4	5	6
Month	Jan	Feb	Mar	Apr	May	June
Sales	27	30	31	27	35	40

Period	7	8	9	10	11	12
Month	July	Aug	Sep	Oct	Nov	Dec
Sales	33	37	46	42	45	44

We are using naïve model for the first calculation. Naïve model forecast values by just simply moving the value of the current observation one time period ahead. We will discuss more about use of these models in next chapters. Now let's just concentrate on the calculations.

Model Estimation using Naïve Model

Period	Month	Sales (Y)	Forecast $(\hat{Y})$	Error $Y - \hat{Y}$	Absolute (error) $\lvert Y - \hat{Y} \rvert$	Squared Error $(Y - \hat{Y})^2$	Absolute Percentage Error $\dfrac{\lvert Y - \hat{Y} \rvert}{Y}$
1	Jan	27	-	-	-	-	-
2	Feb	30	27.00	3.00	3.00	9.00	0.10
3	Mar	31	30.00	1.00	1.00	1.00	0.03
4	Apr	27	31.00	-4.00	4.00	16.00	0.15
5	May	35	27.00	8.00	8.00	64.00	0.23
6	June	40	35.00	5.00	5.00	25.00	0.13
7	July	33	40.00	-7.00	7.00	49.00	0.21
8	Aug	37	33.00	4.00	4.00	16.00	0.11
9	Sep	46	37.00	9.00	9.00	81.00	0.20
10	Oct	42	46.00	-4.00	4.00	16.00	0.10
11	Nov	45	42.00	3.00	3.00	9.00	0.07
12	Dec	44	45.00	-1.00	1.00	1.00	0.02
				1.55	4.45	26.09	0.12
				BIAS	MAD	MSE	MAPE

BIAS

BIAS value is the average of the error term.

Error term is $Y - \hat{Y}$. It is the difference between the observation (Y) and the forecasted or estimated value ($\hat{Y}$). Now take the sum of these values and then divide by the number of terms.

$$\text{BIAS} = \frac{\sum Y - \hat{Y}}{n} = \frac{17}{11} \approx 1.55$$

MAD

Mean Absolute Deviation is the average of the sum of the absolute error.

$$\text{MAD} = \frac{\sum |Y - \hat{Y}|}{n} = \frac{49}{11} \approx 4.45$$

MSE

Mean Square Error is calculated by taking the average of sum of square error. (Difference between actual and estimated values is the error term).

$$\text{MSE} = \frac{\sum (Y - \hat{Y})^2}{n} = \frac{287}{11} \approx 26.09$$

MAPE

Mean Absolute Percentage Error (MAPE) is the average of the absolute percentage errors. Absolute percentage error is calculated by dividing the absolute error by the real observation.

Example : in the above example let's see how the absolute percentage error for February is calculated.

$$\frac{|Y - \hat{Y}|}{Y} = \frac{3}{30} = 0.1$$

Then sum up each absolute percentage error and take the average.

$$\frac{\sum \frac{|Y - \hat{Y}|}{Y}}{n} = = \frac{1.33}{11} = 0.12$$

Model Estimation using Least Square Method

You should have an idea about regression analysis for better understanding of least square method.

period	month	sales	forecast	error	Absolute Error	Squared Error	Percent Error
1	Jan	27	26.94	0.06	0.06	0.00	0.00
2	Feb	30	28.66	1.34	1.34	1.80	0.04
3	Mar	31	30.38	0.62	0.62	0.38	0.02
4	Apr	27	32.11	-5.11	5.11	26.08	0.19
5	May	35	33.83	1.17	1.17	1.37	0.03
6	June	40	35.55	4.45	4.45	19.76	0.11
7	July	33	37.28	-4.28	4.28	18.31	0.13
8	Aug	37	39.00	-2.00	2.00	4.01	0.05
9	Sep	46	40.73	5.27	5.27	27.81	0.11
10	Oct	42	42.45	-0.45	0.45	0.20	0.01
11	Nov	45	44.17	0.83	0.83	0.68	0.02
12	Dec	44	45.90	-1.90	1.90	3.60	0.04
				0.00	**2.29**	**8.67**	**0.06**
				BIAS	MAD	MSE	MAPE

OLS model $y = 1.723x + 25.21$

Model Estimation using Simple MA 3 months

Period	Month	Sales	3-month MA forecast	Error	Absolute Error	Square Error	Percentage Error
1	Jan	27	-	-	-		
2	Feb	30	-	-	-		
3	Mar	31	-	-	-		
4	Apr	27	29.33	-2.33	2.33	5.44	0.09
5	May	35	29.33	5.67	5.67	32.11	0.16
6	June	40	31.00	9.00	9.00	81.00	0.23
7	July	33	34.00	-1.00	1.00	1.00	0.03
8	Aug	37	36.00	1.00	1.00	1.00	0.03
9	Sep	46	36.67	9.33	9.33	87.11	0.20
10	Oct	42	38.67	3.33	3.33	11.11	0.08
11	Nov	45	41.67	3.33	3.33	11.11	0.07
12	Dec	44	44.33	-0.33	0.33	0.11	0.01
				3.11	**3.93**	**25.56**	**0.10**
				BIAS	MAD	MSE	MAPE

Model Estimation using Simple Moving Average 4 months length

Period	Month	Sales	4-month MA forecast	Error	Absolute Error	Square Error	Percentage Error
1	Jan	27	-	-	-		
2	Feb	30	-	-	-		
3	Mar	31	-	-	-		
4	Apr	27	-	-	-		
5	May	35	28.75	6.25	6.25	39.06	0.18
6	June	40	30.75	9.25	9.25	85.56	0.23
7	July	33	33.25	-0.25	0.25	0.06	0.01
8	Aug	37	33.75	3.25	3.25	10.56	0.09
9	Sep	46	36.25	9.75	9.75	95.06	0.21
10	Oct	42	39.00	3.00	3.00	9.00	0.07
11	Nov	45	39.50	5.50	5.50	30.25	0.12
12	Dec	44	42.50	1.50	1.50	2.25	0.03
				4.78	4.84	33.98	0.12
				BIAS	MAD	MSE	MAPE

Model Estimation using Weighted MA

period	month	sales	3-month WMA forecast	error	ABS(error)	Squared Error	Percent Error
1	Jan	27	-	-	-	-	-
2	Feb	30	-	-	-	-	-
3	Mar	31	-	-	-	-	-
4	Apr	27	30.00	-3.00	3.00	9.00	0.11
5	May	35	28.83	6.17	6.17	38.03	0.18
6	June	40	31.67	8.33	8.33	69.44	0.21
7	July	33	36.17	-3.17	3.17	10.03	0.10
8	Aug	37	35.67	1.33	1.33	1.78	0.04
9	Sep	46	36.17	9.83	9.83	96.69	0.21
10	Oct	42	40.83	1.17	1.17	1.36	0.03
11	Nov	45	42.50	2.50	2.50	6.25	0.06
12	Dec	44	44.17	-0.17	0.17	0.03	0.00
				2.56	3.96	25.85	0.10
				BIAS	MAD	MSE	MAPE

If n is the current month W1 is the weight for the previous month (1), W2 is the weight for 2 months before current month(n-2) and W3 is the weight for 3 months before the current month (n-3). Weights are in the next page.

Weights
W1 =   0.5000
W2 =   0.3333
W3 =   0.1667

Model Estimation using Simple Exponential Smoothing

Simple exponential smoothing has exponentially decreasing weight over months.

Equation for Simple Exponential Smoothing is $Y_t = \alpha Y_t + (1-\alpha) Y_{t-1}$

Alpha =0.5

period	month	sales	forecast	error	ABS(error)	Squared Error	Percent Error
1	Jan	27	27.00	-	-	-	-
2	Feb	30	27.00	3.00	3.00	9.00	0.10
3	Mar	31	28.50	2.50	2.50	6.25	0.08
4	Apr	27	29.75	-2.75	2.75	7.56	0.10
5	May	35	28.38	6.63	6.63	43.89	0.19
6	June	40	31.69	8.31	8.31	69.10	0.21
7	July	33	35.84	-2.84	2.84	8.09	0.09
8	Aug	37	34.42	2.58	2.58	6.65	0.07
9	Sep	46	35.71	10.29	10.29	105.86	0.22
10	Oct	42	40.86	1.14	1.14	1.31	0.03
11	Nov	45	41.43	3.57	3.57	12.76	0.08
12	Dec	44	43.21	0.79	0.79	0.62	0.02
				3.02	**4.04**	**24.64**	**0.11**
				BIAS	**MAD**	**MSE**	**MAPE**

Now we can summarize the Key Performance Indicators of the models or else accuracy measures of models to identify which type of model is best suited to forecast the given variables.

According to the below table OLS method gives the best forecasting model for the given data set.

Models	BIAS	MAD	MSE	MAPE
Trend/ OLS	0.00	2.29	8.67	0.05
Naïve	1.55	4.45	26.09	0.09
Moving Avg (3)	2.56	3.96	25.85	0.08
Exponential Smoothing	2.57	3.85	23.48	0.08

Chapter Two: Stationary Time Series

2.1   What is a stationary time series?

Stationary Time Series

Stationary time series models are time series that the mean and the variance of the variable don't depend on the time. Therefore the mean and variance of a stationary time series are constant. They do not have any periodic fluctuations. A stationary time series is simply a stochastic process with constant mean and variance. There are strong stationary series and weak stationary series.

When the distribution of the time series is same as the lagged time series, then it has a strong form of stationary. When the mean and correlation function of a time series does not change by shift in time it is a weak stationary time series. Auto covariance function is not a function of time.

Stationary series is spread around the mean line in a given range. Below is a graph of a stationary time series. Stationary series spread around the mean line in a given range or given upper and lower limits. It has neither trend nor seasonality.

Non Stationary Time Series

Trend, seasonal, cyclic and random patterned series fall under non stationary series. In order to do predictions on a non stationary series, it should be transformed into a stationary series.

Stochastic Process

Stochastic process is a collection of random variables. Time series with the time variable is a basic type of a stochastic process. It is a model for the analysis. This can also be called as random process

Mean of a stochastic process

$\mu_t = E(y_t)$ Where t= 0, ± 1, ±2..., ±n

Autocovariance of stochastic process

$y_{t,s} = Cov(y_t, y_s)$

$Cov(y_t, y_s) = E(y_t - \mu_t)(y_s - \mu_s)$

Where t,s= 0, ± 1, ±2..., ±n

2.2   How to make a stationary Time Series Model

When a time series is not stationary, it should be turned into a stationary series before estimating a model. Below four techniques are four methods to that can be used to transform a non stationary variable into a stationary one.

1. Decomposition technique
2. Smoothing technique
3. Differencing technique
4. Transforming to log technique

2.2.1   Decomposition Techniques

Decomposition models in time series are used to identify and describe trend and seasonal factors.

Decomposition means to break down into simpler parts. When decomposition models are used, we can identify these patterns/factors separately.

Some seasonal patterns of a time series model can be describe as festive season effects, holiday effects. As an example think that there is a festive season effect on sales of a textiles company, the company cannot clearly identify how its sales behave in long term. Therefore we can use this method to remove seasonal effects of the time series data set and then try to identify what kind of a trend, these sales have in long term (do the sales increase or decrease annually?)

There are two types of decomposition models. They are additive models and multiplicative models.

- Additive model is expressed as: Y = T + S + C + I.
- Multiplicative model is expressed as Y = T * S * C * I.

(Y= Time Series Data , T=Trend , S=seasonal ,C=Cynical , I=Irregular)

Some decomposition models are expressed without cynical patterns. They can be written as below

- Additive: Y = Trend + Seasonal + Irregular
- Multiplicative: Y = Trend * Seasonal * Irregular

When seasonal variation is relatively constant over time additive model is useful. When seasonal variation is increasing over time multiplicative model is useful. Multiplicative models are useful in economic and business data modeling. The aim of analyzing a time series is to understand and identify the patterns in a time series variable, therefore a variable with more observation outputs better results.

As an example in each year Textiles Pvt Ltd sell cloths worth of $30000 in December, where in other months they earn between $15000 to $20000. Then it is a constant seasonal variation. We can use additive model for this data series.

But if the Textiles Pvt Ltd earns $30000 in December 2018, $40000in December 2019, $45000 in December 2020, and earns between $15000 to $20000 every other month, then there is a visible increment of seasonal variation. We can use a multiplicative model for this data series.

When multiplicative model $Y = T * S * C * I$ is transformed into log, then it becomes $\log Y = \log T + \log S + \log C + \log I$.

Graphic method, semi-average method, curve fitting by principles and moving average method are used to measure trend.

2.2.2 Smoothing Methods

There are few types of exponential smoothing

1. Simple exponential smoothing or single exponential smoothing – this is suitable for data sets without trend or seasonal patterns. Uses weighted moving averages with exponentially decreasing weights.

2. Double exponential smoothing - this methods has two steps of exponential smoothing, therefore good for more applicable for data sets which has trend.
3. Triple exponential smoothing – more reliable for time series with parabolic trend and seasonality

Single Exponential Smoothing

Single exponential smoothing is suitable for the models which don't show a clear trend or a seasonal pattern. Exponential smoothing is used for forecasting economics and financial data. If there is a time series without a clear pattern then we can use exponential smoothing. But if there is a clear pattern then we should use moving averages.

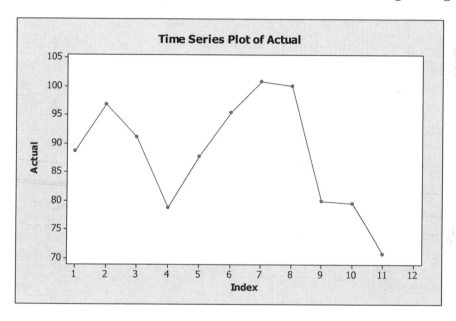

We can use this method to forecast univariate time series. It can be used as an alternative to ARIMA models. While calculating this model past observations get weighted and they are weighted with a geometrically decreasing ratio. Exponential smooth forecasting is a weighted average forecast of past observations.

In single exponential smoothing, smoothing coefficient is called alpha α. Alpha is always between 0 to 1. Smaller alpha values indicate that there is more impact from past observations. Values close to 1 indicates that only most recent past observations has an influence on the predictions. Alpha is the smoothing constant. Alpha is normally selected between 0.1 and 0.3 in practical calculations.

Note: univariate data series is a data series with a single variable. The observations of these data series are recorded according to the time. Example: Annual inflation rate of USA.

Double Exponential Smoothing
Double exponential smoothing is more applicable for univariate data series with trend.
Double exponential smoothing has alpha α and also an additional smoothing factor called β. Double exponential smoothing with additive trend is referred as Holt's linear trend model. Double exponential smoothing with an exponential trend is used for the data series with multiplicative trend. These smoothing techniques are used to remove the trend and make the line straight. This method of making the line straight is called damping in time series. This idea was introduced by Gardner & McKenzie in1985.

Triple Exponential Smoothing
Triple exponential smoothing can be used for univariate seasonal time series. In addition to alpha α and beta β parameters, an additional parameter called gamma γ is used in this method. Gamma is used to control the influence of the seasonal components.

Example 2.1 : Simple exponential smoothing

We use this equation for simple exponential smoothing $\hat{y}_{t+1} = \alpha \, y_t + (1-\alpha) \, F_t$
$\alpha = 0.2$

year	Time	Actual (y_t)	Forecast (F_t)	
1991	1	88.61	89.77	given
1992	2	96.92		
1993	3	91.12		
1994	4	78.75		
1995	5	87.82		
1996	6	95.39		
1997	7	100.88		
1998	8	100.09		
1999	9	79.89		
2000	10	79.59		
2001	11	70.68		
2002	12			

Second forecast value is calculated as below

$\hat{y}_{t+1} = \alpha\, y_t + (1-\alpha)\, F_t$

$\hat{y}_2 = \alpha\, y_1 + (1-\alpha)\, F_1$

$\hat{y}_2 = (0.2* 88.61) + (0.8 *89.77)$

$\hat{y}_2 = $ 89.54

Third forecast value is calculated as below

$\hat{y}_3 = \alpha\, y_2 + (1-\alpha)\, F_2$

$\hat{y}_2 = (0.2* 96.92) + (0.8 *89.54)$

$\hat{y}_2 = 91.016$

Final forecast value (for 2002) is calculated as below

$\hat{y}_{12} = \alpha\, y_{11} + (1-\alpha)\, F_{11}$

$\hat{y}_{12} = (0.2* 70.68) + (0.8 *88.63)$

$\hat{y}_2 = 85.04$

Year	Time	Actual	Forecast
1991	1	88.61	89.77
1992	2	96.92	89.54
1993	3	91.12	91.01
1994	4	78.75	91.04
1995	5	87.82	88.58
1996	6	95.39	88.43
1997	7	100.88	89.82
1998	8	100.09	92.03
1999	9	79.89	93.64
2000	10	79.59	90.89
2001	11	70.68	88.63
2002	12		85.04

We use equation $S_t' = \alpha\, y_{t-1} + (1-\alpha)\, S_{t-1}$ for the double exponential smoothing.

Example 2.2 : Double Moving Average

MA=3

Time	Original Data	S_t'	S_t''	a_t	b_t	F_{t+m}
1	13					
2	8					
3	15	12				
4	4	9				
5	4	7.6	9.53	5.67	-3.86	
6	12	6.7	7.8	5.6	-2.2	1.81
7	11	9	7.8	10.2	2.4	3.4
8	7	10	8.6	11.4	2.8	12.6
9	14	10.7	9.9	11.5	1.6	14.2
10	12	11	10.6	11.4	0.8	13.1

$S_t' = \dfrac{y_t + y_{t-1} + y_{t-2}}{N}$

$S_t' = \dfrac{13+8+15}{3}$

$S_3' = 12$

$S_t'' = \dfrac{S_t' + S_{t-1}' + S_{t-2}'}{N}$

$S_t' = \dfrac{12+9+7.6}{3}$

$S_5' = 9.53$

$a_t = 2S_t' - S_t''$

$a_t = (2*7.6) - 9.53$

$a_5 = 5.67$

$b_t = 2(S_t' - S_t'')$

$b_t = 2(7.6 - 9.53)$

$b_5 = -3.86$

$F_{t+m} = a_{t-1} + m b_{t-1}$

m = number of periods to be forecasted. Here it is taken as 1 time back.
Second forecast value is calculated as below

$F_{t+m} = a_{t-1} + m b_{t-1}$

$F_{t+m} = 5.67 + (-3.86) = 1.81$

2.2.3 Differencing

Differencing is a method of transforming a time series dataset. It can be used to remove the temporal dependencies of time series on time. First differenced model assumes original series has constant average trend or Average trend of original time series is constant. Second differenced models assume original time series has time varying trend. Differencing helps to stabilize the mean of time series by eliminating or reducing trend and seasonality. It is a method of transforming a non stationary time series into a stationary one.

2.2.4 Transforming to log

Transforming to log in time series is a data transformation method. It replaces variable x with log (x). It eliminates/reduces skewness of original data, which turn the series into a normal one. It effectively removes the exponential variance of original time series. It helps to make highly skewed time series to a less skewed one.

Chapter Three: Serial Correlation

3.1   Autocorrelation/ Serial Correlation

Autocorrelation is used to identify non-random observations in a time series. Auto correlation is the correlation inside the same variable during two different successive time intervals. This same concept is also considered as the serial correlation. It is important to identify presence autocorrelation in order to apply a suitable model for the data series. Notation of Greek letter ⍴ is used to represent the autocorrelation.

Autocorrelation reveals the repeating patterns. Correlation is calculated between time series and lagged version of the same time series. This reveals the relationship between current value and past values of the variable.

If $⍴_k$ = 1 , observations departed by lag of k units have a strong positive linear correlation.

If $⍴_k$ = -1 , observations departed by lag of k units have a strong negative linear correlation

If $⍴_k$ is zero then the distribution of $⍴_k$ is Gaussian.

Distribution of autocorrelation when ρ = 0 then $\gamma_k \sim N(0, \frac{1}{n})$

When ρ goes to Zero , γ_k is normally distributed with zero mean and $(\frac{1}{n})$ variance.

Autocorrelation ranges from -1 to +1 (-1 $\leq ⍴_k \leq$ +1). -1 shows a perfect negative auto correlation while +1 shows perfect positive autocorrelation. Autocorrelation can be calculated using below equations.

Autocorrelation coefficient at lag k is

$ρ_k = \frac{r_k}{r_0}$

r_0 -vaiance of time series

r_k - auto covariance function

$ρ_k$ - autocorrelation function

r_k is the covariance of x_t and x_{t+k}

$r_k = \text{Cov}\ (x_t + x_{t+k})$

$r_k = E[(x_t\text{-}\mu) +(x_{t+k}\text{ -}\mu)]$

μ – is the mean

$\rho_{t,t-k} = \text{Correlation of } (y_t, y_{t-k}) = \dfrac{Cov\ (y_t y_{t-k})}{\sqrt{Var\ (y_t)Var\ (y_{t-k})}}$

Where x_t , { t=0,1,2,3}

K = 0,1,2,3

t- time period , k-integers , t-k is the "k" order of lagged series

Example 3.1: Autocorrelation

Calculate the autocorrelation coefficient for one lagged data for the original data series given in the below table

Time	Original Data Series(Y)	One Time lag (Y_{t-1})	Y- μ	Y_{t-1} - μ	$(Y- \mu)*$ $(Y_{t-1} - \mu)$	$(Y- \mu)^2$
1	13					9
2	8	13	-2	3	-6	4
3	15	8	5	-2	-10	25
4	4	15	-6	5	-30	36
5	4	4	-6	-6	36	36
6	12	4	2	-6	-12	4
7	11	12	1	2	2	1
8	7	11	-3	1	-3	9
9	14	7	4	-3	-12	16
10	12	14	2	4	8	4
	μ=10				Sum= -27	Sum=144

μ is calculated by taking the mean of each data series.

Sample autocorrelation function

$$\hat{\rho}_k = \gamma_k = \frac{\sum_{i=1}^{n-k}(y_i - \bar{y})(y_{1+k} - \bar{y})}{\sum_{i-b}^{n}(y_i - \bar{y})^2}$$

$$r_1 = \frac{(8-10)(13-10)+(15-10)(8-10)+\cdots+(12-10)(14-10)}{(13-10)^2+(8-10)^2+\cdots+(12-10)^2}$$

$$r_1 = \frac{-27}{144} = \text{-0.1875}$$

The autocorrelation coefficient between the present value and the first lag is weakly and negatively correlated with a value of -0.1875. Autocorrelation coefficient cans be described as below.

$-1 \leq r_k \leq 1$

If r_k = 1 (Observations departed by lag of k units have a strong positive linear correlation.)

If r_k = -1(Observations departed by lag of k units have a strong negative linear correlation.)

Example 3.2: Autocorrelation

Calculate the autocorrelation coefficient for two lagged data for the original data series given in the below table

Time	Original Data (y)	Original Data Series(Y)	One Time lag (Y_{t-2})	Y- μ	Y_{t-2} - μ	$(Y-μ)*$ $(Y_{t-2} - μ)$
1	13					9
2	8					4
3	15	13	5	3	15	25
4	4	8	-6	-2	12	36
5	4	15	-6	5	-30	36
6	12	4	2	-6	-12	4
7	11	4	1	-6	-6	1
8	7	12	-3	2	-6	9
9	14	11	4	1	4	16
10	12	7	2	-3	-6	4
	μ=10				Sum=-29	Sum= 144

$$r_1 = \frac{(13-10)(15-10)+(8-10)(4-10)+\cdots+(7-10)(12-10)}{(13-10)^2+(8-10)^2+\cdots+(12-10)^2}$$

$$r_1 = \frac{-29}{144} = -0.201$$

Autocorrelation coefficient is (-0.201)

3.2   ACF and PACF

Autocorrelation Function and Partial Autocorrelation Function can determine the best fitted model for given time series. Both functions show the relationship among the observations of a time series. Autocorrelation function calculates the correlation between data series of values that are k interval apart. Partial autocorrelation function calculates the correlation between data series of values that are k interval apart and while doing it, it considers the effect of the values that are between the intervals.

ACF shows if a series is random , seasonal or if it is stationary. Autocorrelation function can be calculated between adjacent entries of a time series.
The autocorrelation order of adjacent entries is presented as one lagged autocorrelation. It has order of k=1. Autocorrelation calculated between each entry and the second entry from it has order of k=2. Order of autocorrelation calculated between each entry and third entry from it is k=3.

Autocorrelation at lag k can be presented as below

$$\rho_k = \frac{Cov\ (Y_t, Y_{t-k})}{\sqrt{V\ (Y_t), V\ (Y_{t-k})}}$$

Foot note : lag is a passed time period in a time series

Sample autocorrelation coefficient is calculated as an estimator for population correlation coefficient.
When the autocorrelation of ACF model is negative or zero at first lag it is better not to take the differenced series. When lag 1 autocorrelation is and more negative than (-0.5) the series can be over

differenced. Over differencing happens when apply differencing at unnecessary occasions such as applying differencing when autocorrelation of 1st lag is zero or nagtive or else when auto correlations of all lags are small or patternless. Overdifferenced series might look random but it might show some patterns if closely examined.

Sample: 1 34
Included observations: 34

Autocorrelation	Partial Correlation		AC	PAC	Q-Stat	Prob
		1	0.462	0.462	7.9205	0.005
		2	0.175	-0.049	9.0908	0.011
		3	-0.010	-0.092	9.0951	0.028
		4	-0.114	-0.084	9.6217	0.047
		5	-0.393	-0.377	16.134	0.006
		6	-0.448	-0.182	24.911	0.000
		7	-0.214	0.125	26.986	0.000
		8	-0.048	0.017	27.096	0.001
		9	0.087	0.087	27.464	0.001
		10	0.029	-0.225	27.505	0.002
		11	0.192	0.058	29.462	0.002
		12	0.094	-0.137	29.949	0.003
		13	0.044	0.044	30.063	0.005
		14	-0.091	-0.046	30.574	0.006
		15	-0.029	0.047	30.628	0.010
		16	-0.092	-0.128	31.200	0.013

Autocorrelation can also be used to find the invertibility of a time series process. We will discuss more on invertibility in coming chapters.

Hypothesis test for ACF
Hypothesis built to test significance of ACF is
$H_0 : \rho_k \neq 0$
$H_0 : \rho_k = 0$

Test statistics $t = \dfrac{\hat{\rho}_k}{\sqrt{1/n}}$, k=1,2,3

Hypothesis test for ρ_k can be done to test if ρ_k is significantly different from zero at each lag. If the hypothesis is rejected then there is no autocorrelation.

Using ACF we can decide if a series is stationary or not (Ex: Slowly dying ACF will suggest there is no stationary). Only ACF cannot be used to identify a suitable model. PACF also be calculated. PACF is useful in identifying the order of the model. MA and AR models can be identified using ACF and PACF functions.

Correlogram No 1

Autocorrelation	Partial Correlation		AC	PAC	Q-Stat	Prob
		1	0.978	0.978	117.79	0.000
		2	0.955	-0.047	231.05	0.000
		3	0.931	-0.034	339.59	0.000
		4	0.903	-0.104	442.59	0.000
		5	0.871	-0.115	539.16	0.000
		6	0.834	-0.124	628.43	0.000
		7	0.799	0.055	711.14	0.000
		8	0.761	-0.094	786.75	0.000
		9	0.720	-0.031	855.22	0.000
		10	0.683	0.047	917.27	0.000
		11	0.646	0.006	973.31	0.000
		12	0.610	0.015	1023.8	0.000
		13	0.575	-0.012	1069.0	0.000
		14	0.540	-0.034	1109.3	0.000
		15	0.505	-0.018	1144.9	0.000
		16	0.473	0.027	1176.4	0.000
		17	0.439	-0.091	1203.8	0.000
		18	0.408	0.052	1227.7	0.000
		19	0.382	0.085	1248.8	0.000
		20	0.355	-0.054	1267.3	0.000
		21	0.329	0.013	1283.3	0.000
		22	0.307	0.062	1297.4	0.000
		23	0.289	0.033	1310.0	0.000
		24	0.272	-0.011	1321.3	0.000
		25	0.253	-0.062	1331.2	0.000
		26	0.238	-0.007	1340.0	0.000
		27	0.224	0.016	1347.9	0.000
		28	0.210	0.002	1354.9	0.000
		29	0.197	-0.026	1361.2	0.000
		30	0.183	-0.025	1366.6	0.000

The correlogram number 1 shows a non-stationary pattern. ACF shows a slowly decaying pattern which is an indication of trend.

Correlogram No 2

		AC	PAC	Q-Stat	Prob
Autocorrelation	Partial Correlation				
		1 0.754	0.754	56.363	0.000
		2 0.440	-0.301	75.698	0.000
		3 0.348	0.366	87.943	0.000
		4 0.455	0.252	109.09	0.000
		5 0.577	0.192	143.48	0.000
		6 0.594	0.136	180.41	0.000
		7 0.503	0.016	207.16	0.000
		8 0.367	-0.090	221.58	0.000
		9 0.244	-0.197	228.03	0.000
		10 0.289	0.204	237.19	0.000
		11 0.490	0.270	263.78	0.000
		12 0.557	-0.120	298.50	0.000
		13 0.382	-0.155	315.00	0.000
		14 0.164	-0.074	318.09	0.000
		15 0.124	0.019	319.88	0.000
		16 0.226	-0.069	325.91	0.000
		17 0.306	-0.035	337.08	0.000
		18 0.281	-0.040	346.57	0.000
		19 0.216	0.079	352.26	0.000
		20 0.093	-0.134	353.34	0.000
		21 0.002	-0.005	353.34	0.000
		22 0.057	0.035	353.75	0.000
		23 0.204	0.030	359.10	0.000
		24 0.257	0.063	367.76	0.000
		25 0.151	0.060	370.78	0.000
		26 0.005	-0.015	370.78	0.000
		27 -0.019	-0.038	370.83	0.000
		28 0.049	-0.038	371.16	0.000
		29 0.104	0.017	372.69	0.000
		30 0.082	-0.113	373.89	0.000
		31 0.049	0.080	374.24	0.000
		32 -0.014	0.033	374.27	0.000

Correlogram no 2 shows that there is a seasonal pattern in the time series variable and the time series is not stationary

Correlogram No 3

		AC	PAC	Q-Stat	Prob
Autocorrelation	Partial Correlation				
		1 0.123	0.123	1.8125	
		2 -0.048	-0.064	2.0933	0.148
		3 0.003	0.018	2.0945	0.351
		4 0.059	0.054	2.5239	0.471
		5 -0.023	-0.037	2.5874	0.629
		6 0.028	0.035	2.6381	0.756
		7 -0.110	-0.124	4.1661	0.654
		8 -0.034	-0.003	4.3169	0.743
		9 -0.005	-0.010	4.3196	0.827
		10 -0.072	-0.079	4.9907	0.835
		11 0.018	0.057	5.0339	0.889
		12 -0.111	-0.145	6.6798	0.824
		13 -0.114	-0.070	8.4061	0.753
		14 -0.006	0.002	8.4111	0.816
		15 -0.004	-0.035	8.4131	0.867
		16 -0.086	-0.060	9.4364	0.854
		17 -0.062	-0.071	9.9670	0.868
		18 0.045	0.063	10.251	0.893
		19 -0.025	-0.073	10.346	0.920
		20 0.215	0.229	16.991	0.590
		21 0.089	0.029	18.130	0.579
		22 0.095	0.088	19.441	0.557
		23 -0.029	-0.054	19.570	0.610
		24 0.147	0.132	22.814	0.472
		25 0.091	0.063	24.070	0.458
		26 0.075	0.030	24.931	0.466
		27 -0.112	-0.071	25.883	0.415
		28 -0.135	-0.141	28.755	0.325
		29 -0.044	-0.042	30.059	0.360
		30 0.036	0.049	30.263	0.401
		31 -0.070	-0.079	31.053	0.413
		32 -0.062	0.024	31.680	0.432
		33 0.026	0.053	31.792	0.477
		34 -0.042	-0.016	32.084	0.513
		35 -0.092	-0.101	33.526	0.491
		36 -0.109	-0.053	35.248	0.456

Correlogram no 3 shows that there is no pattern in the time series and the time series is stationary.

Tips to Consider

If the pattern of ACF and PACF is same, there is a ARMA model.
If the pattern of ACF and PACF of first difference is same, there is an ARIMA model.

3.3   Tests for Serial Correlation

An assumption of time series model is that errors are not serially correlated. In time series model the serial correlation of errors can happen due to correlation within time series and correlation across cross-sectional units.

Although we assume errors are not correlated in time series models, in most of financial time series models, the errors are serially correlated. It happens due to correlation within time series and correlation across cross sectional units.

This violates the assumptions of normal time series models and regression models. There are few tests to identify the significance of the serial correlation.
1. Durbin- Watson d-test
2. Lagrange Multiplier (LM) test
3. Correlograms
4. Ljung –Box (LB) Q statistics

1. Durbin- Watson d-test

D-W test identify the presence of positive autocorrelation.
Hypothesis for D-W test
Hypothesis
$H_0 : \rho=0$
$H_1 : \rho \neq 0$

Test statistic of DW Test

$$d = \frac{\sum_{t=2}^{T}(e_t - e_{t-1})^2}{\sum_{t=1}^{T} e_t^2}$$

where t= 1,2,...T and e_t = Residuals of OLS regression

If DW test statistic is close to 2 then residuals are random. Therefore null hypothesis is not rejected and there is no serial autocorrealtion. Using DW test serial correlation can be calculated for one lag only. (This mean the model is should take form of $y_t = \delta + \beta x_t + u_t$ where the residual are calculated using one lag $u_t = e_1 u_{t-1} + e_t$).If there is no serial correlation between errors $e_1 = 0$ and DW=2

2. Correlograms

Autocorrelation	Partial Correlation		AC	PAC	Q-Stat	Prob
		1	0.123	0.123	1.8125	
		2	-0.048	-0.064	2.0933	0.148
		3	0.003	0.018	2.0945	0.351
		4	0.059	0.054	2.5239	0.471
		5	-0.023	-0.037	2.5874	0.629
		6	0.020	0.035	2.6381	0.756
		7	-0.110	-0.124	4.1661	0.654

Probability of the correlogram is tested under the null hypothesis there is no serial correlation. In the above picture the probability is above the significance level of 5% (Ex : 0.148 > 0.05, 0.351 >0.05 ...) therefore the null hypothesis is not rejected. According to the above picture there is no serial correlation up to 7th lag.

3. Ljung –Box (LB) Q statistics

Hypothesis

H_0 : There is no serial correlation in the residuals upto specified order (k)

H_1 : There is serial correlation in the residuals upto specified order (k)

Or

H_0 : The data are independently distributed

H_1 : The data are not independently distributed

Test Statistic

$$Q = n(n+2) \sum_{k=1}^{h} \frac{\hat{\rho}_k^2}{n-k}$$

$\hat{\rho}_k^2$- autocorrelation at lag k

n- is the sample size

k- lag

the distribution used for this test is chi-square. The rejection region can be shown as $Q > \chi^2_{1-\alpha,h}$ where α is the alpha value and h is the degree of freedom.

Note : Alpha is the value we use to test the significance of the test it shows the acceptability of the type I error. (Please refer to my book Introduction to Hypothesis Testing , if you want to learn more about z-test, t-test,chi-test and f-test.). If P values is higher than the significance value of the confidence level then alternate hypothesis is not rejected.

LB(Q) is used to diagnose serial correlation in the residuals and LB(Q²) is used to diagnose serial correlation in the squared residuals.

4. Breusch Godfrey test

Breusch Godfrey test is based on Lagrange multiplier concept, therefore sometimes this is called as LM test for autocorrelation as well. Breusch Godfery test is based on chi distribution. When the sample is large LM = nR2 ~ χ2(p). Notation for the test statistics of LM test is nR².

Hypothesis

H_0 : There is no serial correlation in the residuals upto specified order (k)

H_1 : There is serial correlation in the residuals upto specified order (k)

Test Statistic

$$LM^* = \frac{n-p-1}{p} \cdot \frac{R^2}{1-R^2} \sim F(p, n-p-1)$$

We can use F distribution to test the test statistic.

P is the regressors; regressors mean the number of variables in a model.

Degree of freedom is n – p– 1. R^2 is the coefficient of determination.

In breusch pagan LM test first we estimate the model using OLS regression

$$y = \beta_0 + \beta_1 x_1 + \cdots + \beta_k x_k + \varepsilon$$

Then we canlculate the residual series

$$e_i = \alpha_0 + \alpha_1 x_{i1} + \cdots + \alpha_k x_{ik} + \rho_1 e_{i-1} + \cdots + \rho_p e_{i-p} + \delta_i$$

Then we test for the serial correlation

This test is better than DW Test as it allows to test higher order of MA and AR process.

Note:

The Lagrange Multiplier (LM) test is a general principle for testing hypotheses about parameters in a likelihood framework. To perform an LM test only estimation of the parameters subject to the restrictions is required. This is in contrast with Wald tests, which are based on unrestricted estimates, and likelihood ratio tests which require both restricted and unrestricted estimates.

3.4   Heteroskedasticity

In ordinary least square method we assume that residuals are constant. Opposite of this assumption is heteroskedasticity. That means there is no constant variance and variance is differencing.

Serial Correlation VS Heteroskedasticity

Serial correlation checks for the autocorrelation between variable at different time periods. But heteroskedasticity means that the value of the variance is not same at every lag or every variable.

Graph 1 Serial Correlation will help to identify the concept of serial correlation and heteroskedasticity.

Graph 1: Serial Correlation

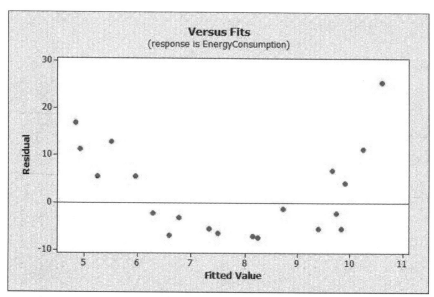

Graph 2: No Serial Correlation

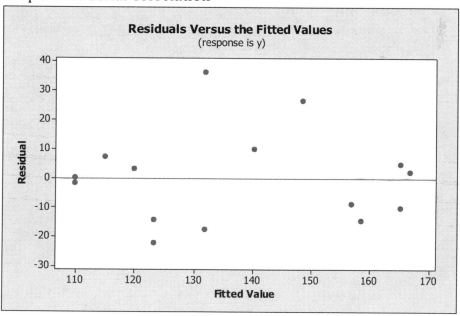

Graph 3: Heteroskedasticity

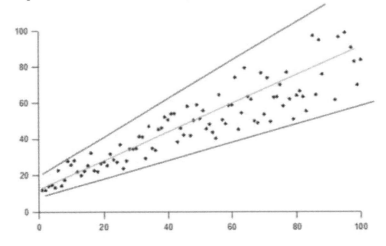

Graph 4: Homoskedasticity

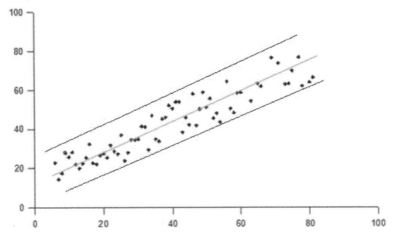

Tests to check heterosckedasticity

1. White test
2. Breusch Pagan test
3. Gold Quandant Test

1. White Test

White test is a common test for heteroskedasticity.

Hypothesis

$H_0 : \sigma_i^2 = \sigma^2$

$H_1 : \sigma_i^2 \neq \sigma^2$

Test statistic

$$F = \frac{\dfrac{R_{\hat{\varepsilon}^2}^2}{1}}{\dfrac{\left(1 - R_{\hat{\varepsilon}^2}^2\right)}{n-2}} \quad \text{or} \quad \chi^2 = nR_{\hat{\varepsilon}^2}^2$$

White test is an asymptotic test and it is suitable for the analysis involving large samples. If it is required for independent variable to have an interactive, non linear effect on the error variance.

In economic data modeling white test for heteroskedasticity is very common.

In white test model for the analysis is calculated using OLS and it looks like below

$$Y_i = \beta_0 + \beta_1 X_{i1} + \dots + \beta_p X_{ip} + \varepsilon_i$$

Then we calculate estimated model and find the residual term.

$$\hat{\varepsilon}_i^2 = \delta_0 + \delta_1 \hat{Y}_i + \delta_2 \hat{Y}_i^2$$

2. Breusch Pagan test

Null hypothesis is that residuals have constant variance.

Hypothesis

$H_0 : \sigma_i^2 = \sigma^2$

$H_1 : \sigma_i^2 \neq \sigma^2$

Test statistic

$$F = \frac{\dfrac{R_{\hat{\varepsilon}^2}^2}{1}}{\dfrac{\left(1 - R_{\hat{\varepsilon}^2}^2\right)}{n-2}} \quad \text{or} \quad \chi^2 = nR_{\hat{\varepsilon}^2}^2$$

In white test model for the analysis is calculated using OLS and it looks like below

$$Y_i = \beta_0 + \beta_1 X_{i1} + \dots + \beta_p X_{ip} + \varepsilon_i$$

Then we calculate estimated model and find the residual term.

$$\hat{\varepsilon}_i^2 = \delta_0 + \delta_1 \hat{Y}_i$$

(Note the difference between residual terms of white test and Breusch Pagan test. White test allows nonlinear effects on residual term)

3. Goldfeld Quandt Test

Goldfield Quandt test is used to test homoskedasticity of regression analysis. It compares the variances of two subgroups. Assumption for the test is "data is normally distributed".

Hypothesis
$$H_0 : \sigma_i^2 = \sigma_2^2$$
$$H_1 : \sigma_i^2 > \sigma_2^2$$

Test statistic

$$GQ = \frac{\hat{\sigma}_1^2}{\hat{\sigma}_2^2} \sim F(n_1 - k_1, n_2 - k_2)$$

3.5 Volatility

Volatility (σ) is the degree of variation of a time series variable, over the time . It is usually measure by the standard deviation of logarithmic returns. Standard deviation or variance can be used to measure volatility. Volatility measures the dispersion of return Large volatility shows that the dispersion of the fluctuation of return is widely spread. Lower volatility indicates the dispersion of fluctuation of return is stead over a period of time and doesn't fluctuate widely.

Volatility is forecasted using heteroskcedasticity models. ARCH and GARCH models are two types of time series models we use to capture volatility of a time series. Purpose of forecasting volatility is to forecast risk in financial matters in order to decide on future investment and returns. By measuring volatility we can take more efficient estimators.

3.6 Unit Root Test

Unit root test is used to test if a time series is stationary or not. Given below the hypothesis used for unit root test.

H_0: There is unit root in time series
H_1: There is no unit root in time series observations
Or
H_0: Time series is not stationary
H_1: Time series is stationary
Or
H_0: $\Phi \geq 1$
H_1: $\Phi < 1$

If there is a unit root in estimated MA coefficients, the forecasting model is considered as non-invertible. If a model is non-invertible residuals of the model doesn't represents the true random noise of the time series model. The null hypothesis of DF test is that there is a unit root in an AR model, which implies that the data series is not stationary.

Augmented Dicky Fuller and Phillips Perron tests are two tests which are commonly used to check the stationary of the variables. Phillips Perron test is widely used in time series analysis.

3.7 Random Walk

Random walk is a time series which is identified as unable to predict. The variable changes of random walk is independent from one period to another. It is a non stationary process. Example: share market price is a random walk. Random walk helps to remove residual auto correlation.

Function of random walk

$y_t = y_{t-1} + z_t$

z_t – discrete random process with mean of μ and variance of σ_z^2

Variance of random walk

$$\text{Var}(y_t) = \text{Var} (e_1 + e_2 + e_3 + \cdots + e_t)$$
$$= \text{Var}(e_1) + \text{Var}(e_2) + \text{Var}(e_3) + \cdots + \text{Var}(e_t)$$
$$= \sigma_e^2 + \sigma_e^2 + \sigma_e^2 + \ldots + \sigma_e^2$$
$$= t\, \sigma_e^2$$

Covariance of random walk

$$\text{Cov}(y_t, y_s) = \text{Cov} (e_1 + e_2 + e_3 + \cdots + e_t)$$
$$= e_1 + e_{t+1} + e_{t+2} + \cdots + e_s$$

Where $1 \le t \le s$ (time is between 1 and s)

$y_{t,s} = \sum_{i=1}^{s} \sum_{j=1}^{t} \text{Cov } e_i, e_j$

When i=j there is covariance

　　If i≠j there is no covariance

Auto correlation function of random walk

$$\rho_{t,s} = \frac{\text{Cov }(y_t\, y_s)}{\sqrt{\text{Var }(y_t)\text{Var }(y_s)}}$$

$\rho_{t,s} = \sqrt{\dfrac{t}{s}}$ where $1 \le t \le s$

Example $\rho_{t,s} = \sqrt{\dfrac{4}{8}} = 0.707$ (here t=4 and s=8)

Chapter Four: ARIMA

4.1 AR

In this chapter, we will be discussing simple and basic yet crucial concepts related to ARIMA model. Before understanding ARIMA model, we should know about AR, MA and ARMA models. Students find these concepts are complicated; therefore I will be discussing the related topics as simple as possible to make it easy for you to understand the necessary information.

Autoregressive (AR) model or Moving Average (MA) models are two important model types in time series analysis.
Autoregressive model is used for building forecasting models when there is some correlation between the values in a time series. In AR model the dependent variable is depending on independent variable plus the previous values of the same dependent variable. AR model is a stochastic process.

AR(p) model is an autoregressive model, where specific lagged values of the dependent variable are used as predictor variable. P is called the order in the model and can be defined as the specific lagged value of the variable.

Model of a general AR(p) process is
$$y_t = \Phi_1 \, y_{t-1} + \Phi_2 \, y_{t-2} + \dots + \Phi_p \, y_{t-p} + e_t$$
e_t or the error term is assumed to be random ,normally and identically distributed(iid).

Time series which have trends or random walks shows strong AR signature. We use differencing to make it stationary. After transforming series using differencing one or two times AR Signature can be changed into MA signature when spikes of the autocorrelation functions become negative.

For non seasonal data series if the stationery series has positive correlation at one lag, AR models fits as the best model. If the stationary series has negative correlation at one lag MA models fits the best.

First order of Autoregressive process AR(1) process. In first order AR model, time is related to <u>one period apart</u> time periods.

The equation of first order AR process, AR(1) is $y_t = \Phi_1 y_{t-1} + e_t$

Φ is vector model coefficient , t is time period and e is residuals.

<u>Autocorrelation function of AR(1)</u>

$$\gamma_0 = \frac{\sigma_e^2}{1 - \emptyset_1^2} \quad \text{Where } \rho_k = \emptyset_1^k, \text{k} = 1,2,3$$

<u>Equation of Second Order AR process AR(2)</u>

$$y_t = \Phi_1 y_{t-1} + \Phi_2 y_{t-2} + e_t$$

<u>Autocorrelation function of AR(2)</u>

$$\gamma_0 = \frac{\sigma^2 (1 - \emptyset_2)}{(1 - \emptyset_2^2 - \emptyset_1^2) - 2\emptyset_1^2 \emptyset_2^2} \quad \text{Where } \rho_k = \emptyset_1^k, \text{k} = 1,2,3$$

<u>Properties of AR (p) process</u>

1. The mean of the y_i in a stationary AR(p) process is

$$\mu = \frac{\phi_0}{1 - \Sigma_{j=1}^{p} \phi_j}$$

2. The variance of the y_i in a stationary AR(1) process is

$$var(y_i) = \frac{\sigma^2}{1 - \phi_1^2}$$

3. The lag h autocorrelation in a stationary AR(1) process is

$$\rho_h = \phi_1^h$$

4.2   MA

Moving Average model uses past forecast errors to build forecast models.

<u>Equation for MA(q) process is as below.</u>

$y_t = \mu + e_t - \theta_1 e_{t-1} - \theta_2 e_{t-2} + \cdots + \theta_t e_{t-q}$

θ_t –coefficients of MA process

e_t - error term

Error Assumption for MA process is $e_t \sim$ iid $N(0, \sigma^2)$, this means error is Purely random process and it is mutually independent and identically distributed. This term is called Gaussian white noise.

Stationary qualities of MA (1)

A stochastic process $\{y_t\}$ t≥1 is said to be strictly stationary if its all moments of order do not depend on the time.

A stochastic process $\{y_t\}$ t≥1 is said to be weakly stationary if its first two order moments does not depend on the time.

The mean $E(y_t)$ and variance $V(y_t)$ of any MA(q) process are finite and constant, and the autocorrelation function is finite and does not depend on t. Therefore any MA(q) is weakly stationary.

MA(1) process is supposed to be always weakly stationary since first two moment are independent of time.

MA(1) > $E(y_t) = 0$, $E(y_t^2) = V(y_t) = (1 + \theta_t^2) \sigma^2$

Properties of MA(q) process

1. The mean of an MA(q) process is μ.

2. The variance of an MA(q) process is
$$var(y_i) = \sigma^2(1 + \theta_1^2 + \cdots + \theta_q^2)$$

3. The autocorrelation function of an MA(1) process is
$$\rho_1 = \frac{\theta_1}{1 + \theta_1^2} \qquad \rho_h = 0 \text{ for } h > 1$$

4. The autocorrelation function of an MA(2) process is
$$\rho_2 = \frac{\theta_1 + \theta_1 \theta_2}{1 + \theta_1^2 + \theta_2^2} \qquad \rho_2 = \frac{\theta_2}{1 + \theta_1^2 + \theta_2^2} \qquad \rho_h = 0 \text{ for } h > 2$$

5. The autocorrelation function of an MA(q) process is
$$\rho_h = \frac{\theta_h + \sum_{j=1}^{q-h} \theta_j \theta_{j+h}}{1 + \sum_{j=1}^{q} \theta_j^2} \qquad \text{for } h \le q \text{ and } \rho_h = 0 \text{ for } h > q$$

6. The PACF of an MA(1) process is

$$\pi_k = \frac{-(-\theta_1)^k}{1 + \sum_{i=1}^{k} \theta_1^{2i}} \qquad \pi_{k,k-j} = \frac{-(-\theta_1)^j}{1 + \sum_{i=1}^{j} \theta_1^{2i}} \cdot \pi_k$$

where $1 \leq j < n$.

Properties of MA(1) with mean zero

- Model for MA(1) is $y_t = e_t - \theta_1 e_{t-1}$
  Where e_t is purely random

- The mean of the MA(1) Process
  $E(y_t) = E(e_t - \theta_1 e_{t-1})$
  $E(y_t) = E(e_t) - \theta_1 E(e_{t-1})$
  $E(y_t) = 0 - \theta_1 0$
  $E(y_t) = 0$

- The variance of MA(1) Process
  $V(y_t) = V(e_t - \theta_1 e_{t-1})$
  $V(y_t) = V(e_t) + \theta_1^2 V(e_{t-1}) + 2\text{Cov}(e_t, e_{t-1})$
  $E(y_t) = \sigma^2 + \theta^2 \sigma^2 + 0$
  $E(y_t) = (1 + \theta_1^2)\sigma^2$

- Covariance of MA(1) Process
  $$\rho_{xy} = \frac{\gamma_{xy}}{\sqrt{v(x)v(y)}}$$
  $$\rho_{xy} = \frac{\gamma_1}{\sqrt{v(y_t)\, v(y_{t-1})}}$$
  $$\rho_{xy} = \frac{\gamma_1}{\sqrt{v(y_t)}}$$
  $$\rho_{xy} = \frac{\gamma_1^2}{\sqrt{(1+\theta_1^2)\, \sigma^2}}$$

AR and MA models can be used to identify the patterns and get forecast values of a time series. AR model uses the data of dependent variable of a time series to forecast. MA model uses error series of the time series to forecast. If the both models are used together it is

49

called ARMA model. It uses both dependent variable and errors for analysis of a time series.

If the data is stationary ARMA model can be used. The generalized term of ARMA model is ARIMA. It can be used for non stationary data as well after taking differences or transforming.

4.3   Backshift Operator

Backshift has the effect of shifting the data back k times of period. Backshift operator is called lag operator. It works on time series and means "back up by one time unit".

Backshift operator is convenient for describing the process of differencing.

First difference is represented by (1-B) y_t

Second difference is represented by $(1 - B)^2 y_t$

In AR (p) Process , Error (e_t) can be express as below.

$e_t = \Phi B_t$ $y_t = \Phi y_{t-1} + e_t$

AR (1) model can be written as below using backshift operator

$e_t =(1- \Phi B)y_t$

AR (2) model can be written as below using backshift operator

$e_t =(1- \Phi_1 B - \Phi_2 B^2)$

Below conditions should be checked on backshift operator to check if the process is stationary.

Stationary Conditions for AR (1)

$\Phi_1 <+1$ (First coefficient is less than +1)

Stationary Conditions for AR (2)

1. $\Phi_2 + \Phi_1 <1$ (Sum of first and second coefficients should be less than +1)
2. $\Phi_2 - \Phi_1 <1$ (Difference between first and second coefficients should be less than +1)
3. $-1 < \Phi_2 <+1$ (Second coefficient is between minus 1 and plus 1)

Example 4.1: Backshift Operator

$y_t = -1.5\ y_{t-1} + 0.4\ y_{t-2} + e_t$ is a stationary model. Above process takes AR(2) signature. This AR(2) process can be written as below using backshift operators

$\Phi B = (1 - \Phi_1 B + \Phi_2 B^2) = e_t$
$\Phi B = (1 - 1.5\ B + 0.7 B^2) = e_t$
Therefore $\Phi_1 = (-1.5)$, $\Phi_2 = (0.7)$

Apply these values for the conditions for the given AR(2) model
1. $\Phi_2 + \Phi_1 < 1$
     $(-1.5) + 0.7 = -0.8\ < 1$
2. $\Phi_2 - \Phi_1 < 1$
     $0.7 - (-1.5) > 1$

3. $-1 < \Phi_2 < +1$
     $-1 < 0.7 < +1$

4.4   Invertibility

Invertibility refers to linear stationary process which behaves like infinite representation of autoregressive. Invertibility solves non-uniqueness of autocorrelation function of moving average.

When AR models can be written as MA or MA models can be written as AR models, it is called an invertible model.

Invertibility of MA(1)

MA(1) model equation is
$y_t = e_t - \theta_t e_{t-1}$ ....(1)
Using backshift operator B can be defined as $B^i e_t = e_{t-j}$
Therefore
$B^0 e_t = B^0 e_t = e_t$
$B^1 e_t = e_{t-1}$

Equation (1) can be written as
$y_t = e_t - \theta_t B e_t$
$y_t = e_t (1 - \theta_1 B)$ ....(2)
Introduce $\Phi(B)$, $y_t = \Phi(B)\ e_t$
$\Phi(B)$ is a function of B

Invertible MA(1) model

$y_t = e_t - \theta_t B e_t$

$y_t = (1 - \theta_B) e_t$ ....(3)   As in equation (2)

As $y_t = \Phi(B) e_t$

And $y_t = e_t (1 - \theta_1 B)$

Then $\theta_t B e_t = e_t (1 - \theta_1 B)$

Equation (3) can be replaced

$y_t = \Phi(B) e_t$

When $\Phi B = 0$

then $(1 - \theta B) = 0$

$1 = \theta B$

$B = \frac{1}{\theta}$

MA (1) to be invertible $\frac{1}{\theta_1} > 1$

Or $\theta_1 < 1$

Invertible MA(2) Model

$y_t = e_t - \theta_1 e_{t-1} - \theta_2 e_{t-2}$

$B^j e_t = e_{t-j}$

$t = 0$, $B^0 e_t = e_{t-0} = e_t$

$t = 1$, $B^1 e_t = e_{t-1}$

$t = 2$, $B^2 e_t = e_{t-2}$

$y_t = e_t - \theta_1 e_{t-1} - \theta_2 e_{t-2}$

$y_t = e_t - \theta_1 B e_{t-1} - \theta_2 B^2 e_t$

$y_t = e_t (1 - \theta_1 B - \theta_2 B^2)$

$\Phi B = 1 - 1 - \theta_1 B - \theta_2 B^2$

Then

$y_t = e_t - \theta_1 e_{t-1} - \theta_2 e_{t-2}$

$y_t = e_t (1 - \theta_1 B - \theta_2 B^2)$

When $\Phi B = 0$

$1 - \theta_1 B - \theta_2 B^2 = 0$

$1 = \theta_1 B - \theta_2 B^2$

$\theta_2 B^2 + \theta_1 B - 1 = 0$

$$B = \frac{-\theta_1 \pm \sqrt{\theta^2\ 4\theta\ (-1)}}{2\theta_2}$$

$$\frac{-\theta_1 \pm \sqrt{\theta_1^2 + 4\theta_2}}{2\theta_2} > 1$$

To make MA(2) invertible roots of

$(1 - \theta_1 B - \theta_2 B^2 = 0) > 1$

$\theta_1 + \theta_2 < 0$

$\theta_2 - \theta_1 < 0$

$-1 < \theta_2 < 1$

Thus, the process is invertible when $|\theta| < 1$ $|\theta| < 1$.
The invertibility constraints for other models are similar to the stationarity constraints.

For an MA(1) model: $-1 < \theta 1 < 1$, $-1 < \theta 1 < 1$.
For an MA(2)
model: $-1 < \theta 2 < 1$, $-1 < \theta 2 < 1$, $\theta 2 + \theta 1 > -1$, $\theta 2 + \theta 1 > -1$, $\theta 1 - \theta 2 < 1 \theta 1 - \theta 2 < 1$

Example 4.2 : Invetibility
1. Derive ACF of the $y_t = (1 - 0.6\ B)\ e_t$

   $y_t = (1 - 0.6\ B)\ e_t$
   $y_t = (e_t - 0.6\ Be_t)$
   $y_t = e_t - 0.6\ Be_{t-1}$
   In the above equation $\theta_1 = 0.6$. Therefore this is a MA (1)
   signature model as there is one θ value

This above value of Θ can be substitute to below equation of ACF
(Lag order is k=1)

$$\rho_k = \begin{cases} \dfrac{-\theta_1}{1+\theta_1^2}, & i+k=1 \\ 0, & otherwise \end{cases}$$

$$\rho_k = \begin{cases} \dfrac{-0.6}{1+0.36} \\ 0 \end{cases}$$

2. Is $y_t = (1\text{-}0.6\ B)\ e_t$ invertible?

1-0.6 B=0

$B=\dfrac{1}{0.6}$

B=1.6

B>1

This implies roots of θ_B lie outside the unit order. That implies y_t is invertible.

3. Derive ACF of $y_t = (1\text{-}\ 1.2B + 0.35\ B^2\ )\ e_t$

$y_t = (1\text{-}\ 1.2B + 0.35\ B^2\ )\ e_t$
$y_t = (e_t\text{-}\ 1.2B\ e_t + 0.35\ B^2 e_t\ )$
$y_t = (e_t - \theta_1 B\ e_{t-1}\text{-}\ \theta_2\ B^2 e_{t-2}\ )$

$\theta_1 = 1.2 \qquad \theta_2 = \text{-}0.35$

This is a model with MA(2) signature because there are θ_1 and θ_2.
Substitute θ_1 and θ_2 to the properties.

$$\rho_2 = \begin{cases} \dfrac{-\theta_1 + \theta_1\theta_2}{1 + \theta_1^2 + \theta_2^2} & k=1 \\ \dfrac{-\theta_2}{1 + \theta_1 + \theta_2^2} & k=2 \\ 0 & otherwise \end{cases}$$

$$\rho_2 = \begin{cases} \dfrac{-1.2+(1.2)(-0.35)}{1+1.2^2+0.35^2} & k = 1 \\ \dfrac{-(-0.35)}{1+1.2^2+0.35^2} & k = 2 \\ 0 & otherwise \end{cases}$$

Check if $y_t = (1- 1.2B+ 0.35\ B^2)\ e_t$ is invertible
For invertible process , roots of ΦB , of $y=\Phi B$ should lie outside the unit circle.

$(1-1.2B + 0.35\ B^2) > 1$

$\theta_1 + \theta_2 < 1$

$\theta_2 - \theta_1 < 1$

Condition of $-1 < \theta_2 < 1$ needs to be satisfied to be invertible.

$\theta_2 = -0.35$

$\theta_1 = 1.2$

Apply above values to below equations.

$\theta_1 + \theta_2 < 1$, $1.2 - 0.35 < 1$

$\theta_2 - \theta_1 < 1$, $(-0.35)- 1.2 < 1$

$\theta_2 = 0.35$ lies $-1 < \theta_2 < 1$, this implies $y_t = (1- 1.2B+ 0.35\ B^2)\ e_t$ is invertible

Example 4.3 : MA(1) Model
Find the data sets for given examples in excel sheet at
https://www.facebook.com/groups/590090104970492/files   or
my website
http://www.anushabooks.com/documents/TimeSeriesAnalysisExam
ples.xlsx Dataset for this example is named as MA1. (Please not that
sometimes the outputs can be bit differed according to the software
version)

E-views steps : Import excel file > open "sales" data series >view >
graph
The graph in next page of sales shows that there is upward trend in
sales for 25 years.

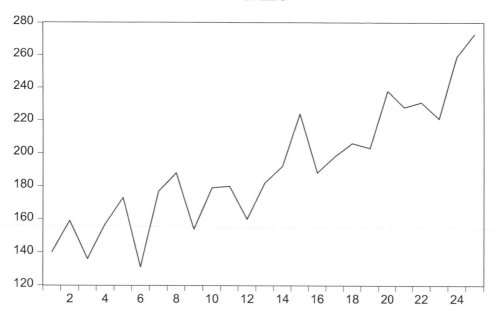

SALES

E views : views > descriptive stats and tests > stats table

	SALES
Mean	191.08
Median	188
Maximum	273
Minimum	131
Std. Dev.	37.39086
Skewness	0.37799
Kurtosis	2.488564
Jarque-Bera	0.867782
Probability	0.647983
Sum	4777
Sum Sq. Dev.	33553.84
Observations	25

The average sales for 25 months is 191.08 dollars, with a minimum of 131 dollars and maximum of 273 dollars. Jarque Bera statistics shows that the data series is normally distributed.

E views : views > unit root test> level

	t-Statistic	Prob.*
Null Hypothesis: SALES has a unit root Exogenous: Constant Lag Length: 2 (Automatic - based on SIC, maxlag=5)		
Augmented Dickey-Fuller test statistic	0.478730	0.9818
Test critical values: 1% level	-3.769597	
5% level	-3.004861	
10% level	-2.642242	
*MacKinnon (1996) one-sided p-values.		

Null Hypothesis: SALES has a unit root

Null hypothesis is not rejected. Therefore that indicates the time series is not stationary. Therefore let's take the differenced series.

Select "Differenced" after drawing the graph in e-views. There is a dropdown list on the top of the graph output. You can find the word differenced in the dropdown list. Differenced data series seems to be stationary as it is closely spread around zero line.

Differenced SALES

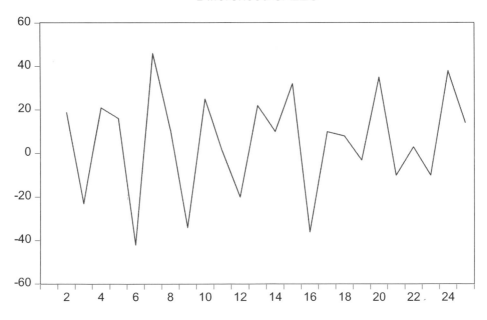

	Sales	DSALES
Mean	191.08	5.541667
Std. Dev.	37.39086	23.94192
Skewness	0.37799	-0.40309
Kurtosis	2.488564	2.361227
Jarque-Bera	0.867782	1.057943
Probability	0.647983	0.589211
Observations	25	24

E views : views > unit root test> 1st difference

Null Hypothesis: D(SALES) has a unit root Exogenous: Constant Lag Length: 1 (Automatic - based on SIC, maxlag=5)		
	t-Statistic	Prob.*
Augmented Dickey-Fuller test statistic	-6.911113	0.0000
Test critical values: 1% level	-3.769597	
5% level	-3.004861	
10% level	-2.642242	
*MacKinnon (1996) one-sided p-values.		

Null Hypothesis of fist difference of SALES (D(SALES)) has a unit root is rejected. Therefore that indicates the time series is stationary. Now we can find a model for this differenced series.

Correlogram of ACF and PACF
Eviews : views> correlogram> level 1

Sample: 1 25
Included observations: 24

Autocorrelation	Partial Correlation		AC	PAC	Q-Stat	Prob
		1	-0.471	-0.471	6.0094	0.014
		2	-0.173	-0.506	6.8543	0.032
		3	0.329	-0.054	10.080	0.018
		4	-0.264	-0.243	12.252	0.016
		5	0.077	-0.096	12.447	0.029
		6	0.079	-0.088	12.665	0.049
		7	0.092	0.335	12.976	0.073
		8	-0.154	0.157	13.901	0.084
		9	-0.118	-0.116	14.476	0.106
		10	0.217	-0.103	16.573	0.084
		11	-0.044	0.080	16.665	0.118
		12	-0.125	-0.102	17.476	0.133

In autocorrelation graph the first lag is significant. In PACF two lags are significant.

ACF is used to identify the AR signature. As there is 1 lag which is significant, we can apply up to AR(1) signature. PACF is used to identify MA signature, as there are two lags which are significant in PACF, we can apply MA(2) signature.

Before selecting one model we should test few models on the same dataset. Postulate models are the parsimonious models, which means all the possible models which can be applied for a data series.

In this data series, we can apply

1. AR(1) MA(1)
2. AR(1) MA(2)
3. We can also apply AR(1) , MA(1) and MA(2) Models Separately

It is not necessary to explain about all applications of the models in a research or in an exercise unless requested. But for your learning experience , I will be talking about application of few extra models.

AR(1) MA(1)

E views : Quick > Estimate equation > type the equation in space: d(sales) c ar(1) ma(1)

Dependent Variable: D(SALES)
Method: Least Squares
Sample (adjusted): 3 25
Included observations: 23 after adjustments
Convergence achieved after 20 iterations
MA Backcast: 2

Variable	Coefficient	Std. Error	t-Statistic	Prob.
C	4.775923	0.921679	5.181764	0.0000
AR(1)	-0.163303	0.248394	-0.657436	0.5184
MA(1)	-0.905714	0.163466	-5.540678	0.0000

R-squared	0.522138	Mean dependent var		4.956522
Adjusted R-squared	0.474352	S.D. dependent var		24.30391
S.E. of regression	17.62072	Akaike info criterion		8.697136
Sum squared resid	6209.797	Schwarz criterion		8.845244
Log likelihood	-97.01706	Hannan-Quinn criter.		8.734385
F-statistic	10.92654	Durbin-Watson stat		1.875657
Prob(F-statistic)	0.000621			

Inverted AR Roots	-.16
Inverted MA Roots	.91

Since the AR(1) process is not significant (p-value $0.5184 > 0.05$) at 5% of significance level , we should test for MA(1) model without AR(1).

E views : Quick > Estimate equation > type the equation in space:
d(sales) c ma(1)

MA(1) Model

Dependent Variable: D(SALES)
Method: Least Squares
Sample (adjusted): 2 25
Included observations: 24 after adjustments
Convergence achieved after 44 iterations
MA Backcast: OFF (Roots of MA process too large)

Variable	Coefficient	Std. Error	t-Statistic	Prob.
C	5.435948	0.991777	5.481020	0.0000
MA(1)	-1.574901	0.299221	-5.263344	0.0000

R-squared	0.759579	Mean dependent var	5.541667
Adjusted R-squared	0.748651	S.D. dependent var	23.94192
S.E. of regression	12.00322	Akaike info criterion	7.887883
Sum squared resid	3169.702	Schwarz criterion	7.986054
Log likelihood	-92.65459	Hannan-Quinn criter.	7.913928
F-statistic	69.50610	Durbin-Watson stat	2.387751
Prob(F-statistic)	0.000000		

Inverted MA Roots	1.57
Estimated MA process is noninvertible	

According to the above table MA(1) parameter is significant (p-value <0.05) at 5% of significance level. R-square value is 0.76 , this is less than AR(1) MA(1) model. In most cases R-Square value is not that considered. (For time series, Stationary R-squared is preferable to ordinary R-squared when there are trends or seasonal patterns. In order to select the best fit model, the model with the lowest MAE or RMSE value should be selected.) F statistic is also significant. AIC value is 7.88.

AR(1) MA(2)

We should then check for AR(1) MA(2) Model

E views : Quick > Estimate equation > type the equation in space:
d(sales) c ar(1) ma(2)

Dependent Variable: D(SALES)
Method: Least Squares
Sample (adjusted): 3 25
Included observations: 23 after adjustments
Convergence achieved after 19 iterations
MA Backcast: 1 2

Variable	Coefficient	Std. Error	t-Statistic	Prob.
C	4.864724	0.791257	6.148099	0.0000
AR(1)	-0.702648	0.163586	-4.295290	0.0004
MA(2)	-0.878557	0.125536	-6.998475	0.0000

R-squared	0.560526	Mean dependent var	4.956522
Adjusted R-squared	0.516578	S.D. dependent var	24.30391
S.E. of regression	16.89815	Akaike info criterion	8.613393
Sum squared resid	5710.949	Schwarz criterion	8.761501
Log likelihood	-96.05402	Hannan-Quinn criter.	8.650642
F-statistic	12.75446	Durbin-Watson stat	2.215844
Prob(F-statistic)	0.000269		

Inverted AR Roots	-.70	
Inverted MA Roots	.94	-.94

AR(1) and MA(2) model is also significant.

According to the above table AR(1)MA(2) parameters are significant (p-value <0.05) at 5% of significance level. R-square value is 0.56 , this is less than MA(1) model. F statistic is also significant. AIC value is 8.6.

Comparing both the models MA(1) model has less AIC value and high R-squared value. R –squared value shows how much the fitted line represents the observed data. Higher r square value is better. Therefore for the above data set MA(1) model fits better.

Now let's check for residual tests.

E views : Quick > Estimate equation > type the equation in space:

d(sales) c ma(1)

Sample: 1 25
Included observations: 24

Autocorrelation	Partial Correlation		AC	PAC	Q-Stat	Prob
		1	-0.192	-0.192	1.0025	0.317
		2	-0.166	-0.211	1.7877	0.409
		3	0.068	-0.013	1.9243	0.588
		4	0.088	0.072	2.1656	0.705
		5	-0.194	-0.159	3.4055	0.638
		6	-0.136	-0.208	4.0511	0.670
		7	0.165	0.026	5.0484	0.654
		8	0.131	0.148	5.7212	0.678
		9	-0.011	0.137	5.7265	0.767
		10	0.012	0.072	5.7334	0.837
		11	-0.036	-0.100	5.7957	0.887
		12	-0.163	-0.238	7.1831	0.845

Null Hypothesis: Residuals are random

P value of q statistics up to 12 lags are not significant (see the probability column in the above chart). Therefore the null hypothesis is not rejected. Residuals are random.

Eviews: View > residual diagnostic > histogram -normality

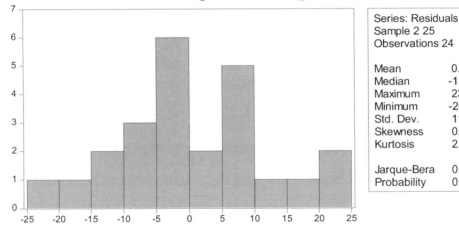

Series: Residuals	
Sample 2 25	
Observations 24	
Mean	0.839093
Median	-1.346638
Maximum	23.11230
Minimum	-20.51633
Std. Dev.	11.70805
Skewness	0.057967
Kurtosis	2.384705
Jarque-Bera	0.392028
Probability	0.822001

Null Hypothesis : Residuals are normally distributed. Jarque Bera test statistic is used to test the normality of residuals. P-value of JB statistic is 0.822 , which is higher than 0.05. Therefore null hypothesis is not rejected. Residuals are normally distributed. In time series analysis testing correlation is important as if there is serial correlation left in residuals, it means there still are unexplained effects left in time series, and hence volatility models (GARCH/ARCH) should be fitted.

Breusch-Godfrey Serial Correlation LM Test:			
F-statistic	2.769837	Prob. F(12,10)	0.0581
Obs*R-squared	18.41958	Prob. Chi-Square(12)	0.1035

Null hypothesis: There is no serial correlation in the residuals upto lag order 12. Null hypothesis is not rejected (p-value =0.0581 >0.05). Therefore there is no serial correlation. (Note that if we take lag order two , this test will be significant, if we take lag order 24, then the p value will be near to a singular matrix value. We should enter the highest number that we expect serial correlation to be possible)

The MA(1) model for the dataset is

$$y_t = e_t - 1.5749\ e_{t-1}\ (y_t = e_t - \theta_1 e_{t-1})$$

Example 4.4: AR(1)

E-views steps : Import excel file > open "Y" data series >view > graph. Although there are some fluctuation the graph doesn't show any trend or any pattern. The graph shows that data can be stationary. We need to do significance tests to confirm this assumption.

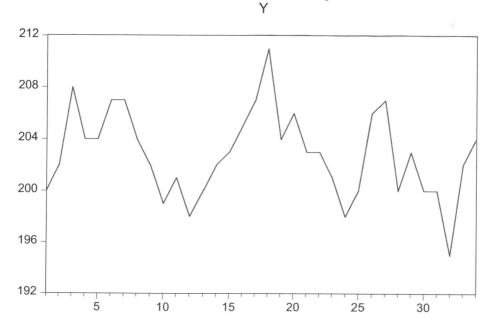

Y

The data series is normally distributed according to Jarque Bera test. Mean of Y variable is 202.8235 and Median is 203. Maximum value of Y series is 211 and minimum value of Y series is 195. You can also describe about range, kurtosis and skewness here.

Descriptive Statistics	Y
Mean	202.8235
Median	203
Maximum	211
Minimum	195
Std. Dev.	3.370735
Skewness	0.121022
Kurtosis	2.923593

Descriptive Statistics	Y
Jarque-Bera	0.091267
Probability	0.955392
Sum	6896
Sum Sq. Dev.	374.9412
Observations	34

Sample: 1 34
Included observations: 34

Autocorrelation	Partial Correlation		AC	PAC	Q-Stat	Prob
		1	0.462	0.462	7.9205	0.005
		2	0.175	-0.049	9.0908	0.011
		3	-0.010	-0.092	9.0951	0.028
		4	-0.114	-0.084	9.6217	0.047
		5	-0.393	-0.377	16.134	0.006
		6	-0.448	-0.182	24.911	0.000
		7	-0.214	0.125	26.986	0.000
		8	-0.048	0.017	27.096	0.001
		9	0.087	0.087	27.464	0.001
		10	0.029	-0.225	27.505	0.002
		11	0.192	0.058	29.462	0.002
		12	0.094	-0.137	29.949	0.003
		13	0.044	0.044	30.063	0.005
		14	-0.091	-0.046	30.574	0.006
		15	-0.029	0.047	30.628	0.010
		16	-0.092	-0.128	31.200	0.013

Auto correlation function shows there can be a AR(1) signature and the partial correlation function has MA(1) signature. Autocorrelation Function shows a negative spike. Therefore It is possible this dataset has MA(1) order

		t-Statistic	Prob.*
Null Hypothesis: Y has a unit root			
Exogenous: Constant			
Lag Length: 0 (Automatic - based on SIC, maxlag=8)			

		t-Statistic	Prob.*
Augmented Dickey-Fuller test statistic		-3.408032	0.0178
Test critical values:	1% level	-3.646342	
	5% level	-2.954021	
	10% level	-2.615817	

*MacKinnon (1996) one-sided p-values.

STATIONARY

H_0 : Y has a unit root

H_1 : Y doesn't have a unit root

Ho is rejected. Therefore we can conclude that the time series is stationary.

Now we can try to fit a model.

Dependent Variable: Y
Method: Least Squares
Sample (adjusted): 2 34
Included observations: 33 after adjustments
Convergence achieved after 70 iterations
MA Backcast: 1

Variable	Coefficient	Std. Error	t-Statistic	Prob.
C	202.9994	0.983449	206.4157	0.0000
AR(1)	0.416450	0.335865	1.239931	0.2246
MA(1)	0.063750	0.373404	0.170726	0.8656

R-squared	0.220844	Mean dependent var	202.9091
Adjusted R-squared	0.168900	S.D. dependent var	3.385296
S.E. of regression	3.086194	Akaike info criterion	5.178262
Sum squared resid	285.7378	Schwarz criterion	5.314309
Log likelihood	-82.44133	Hannan-Quinn criter.	5.224038
F-statistic	4.251594	Durbin-Watson stat	1.982356
Prob(F-statistic)	0.023679		

Inverted AR Roots	.42
Inverted MA Roots	-.06

AR(1) and MA(1) signature is not significant when used in combination. Let's check both signatures separately.

Dependent Variable: Y
Method: Least Squares
Sample: 1 34
Included observations: 34
Convergence achieved after 14 iterations
MA Backcast: 0

Variable	Coefficient	Std. Error	t-Statistic	Prob.
C	202.8187	0.733797	276.3964	0.0000
MA(1)	0.393171	0.163058	2.411233	0.0218

R-squared	0.185374	Mean dependent var	202.8235
Adjusted R-squared	0.159917	S.D. dependent var	3.370735
S.E. of regression	3.089482	Akaike info criterion	5.150906
Sum squared resid	305.4367	Schwarz criterion	5.240692
Log likelihood	-85.56541	Hannan-Quinn criter.	5.181526
F-statistic	7.281842	Durbin-Watson stat	1.804687
Prob(F-statistic)	0.011027		

Inverted MA Roots	-.39

MA(1) signature is significant here according to the above table and the below correlogram confirms it. All the spikes do not go beyond the control limits.

Sample: 1 34
Included observations: 34

Autocorrelation	Partial Correlation		AC	PAC	Q-Stat	Prob
		1	-0.210	-0.210	1.6306	0.202
		2	-0.010	-0.057	1.6348	0.442
		3	-0.153	-0.176	2.5630	0.464
		4	-0.026	-0.107	2.5898	0.629
		5	-0.136	-0.201	3.3729	0.643
		6	0.251	0.152	6.1363	0.408
		7	-0.147	-0.115	7.1119	0.417
		8	0.142	0.075	8.0638	0.427
		9	-0.055	0.015	8.2146	0.513
		10	-0.095	-0.127	8.6708	0.564
		11	-0.112	-0.108	9.3327	0.591
		12	0.146	0.025	10.512	0.571
		13	-0.173	-0.154	12.258	0.507
		14	0.344	0.235	19.491	0.147
		15	0.105	0.260	20.206	0.164
		16	-0.168	-0.097	22.135	0.139

Graph in next page shows that the residuals are normally distributed of MA(1) model.

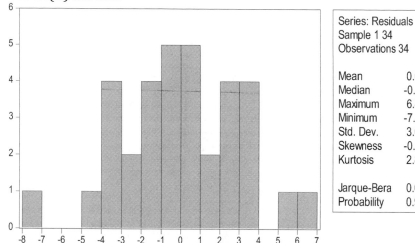

Series: Residuals	
Sample 1 34	
Observations 34	
Mean	0.012382
Median	-0.167979
Maximum	6.853262
Minimum	-7.250306
Std. Dev.	3.042285
Skewness	-0.030480
Kurtosis	2.850162
Jarque-Bera	0.037071
Probability	0.981635

Serial correlation test shows that there is no serial correlation in residual term.

Breusch-Godfrey Serial Correlation LM Test:			
F-statistic	1.794173	Prob. F(12,20)	0.1196
Obs*R-squared	17.62604	Prob. Chi-Square(12)	0.1275

If you observed below table , you can see that the AR(1) signature is significant as the p value is 0.0060. Durban Watson test is also near 2.

Dependent Variable: Y
Method: Least Squares
Sample (adjusted): 2 34
Included observations: 33 after adjustments
Convergence achieved after 3 iterations

Variable	Coefficient	Std. Error	t-Statistic	Prob.
C	203.0141	0.989402	205.1886	0.0000
AR(1)	0.464141	0.157234	2.951908	0.0060

R-squared	0.219414	Mean dependent var	202.9091
Adjusted R-squared	0.194234	S.D. dependent var	3.385296
S.E. of regression	3.038793	Akaike info criterion	5.119490
Sum squared resid	286.2621	Schwarz criterion	5.210187
Log likelihood	-82.47158	Hannan-Quinn criter.	5.150006
F-statistic	8.713760	Durbin-Watson stat	1.934760
Prob(F-statistic)	0.005972		

Correlogram shows that the error term is random. (The spikes do not cross or pass the control limits)

Sample: 1 34
Included observations: 33

Autocorrelation	Partial Correlation		AC	PAC	Q-Stat	Prob
		1	-0.186	-0.186	1.2492	0.264
		2	-0.004	-0.040	1.2498	0.535
		3	-0.180	-0.195	2.4930	0.477
		4	0.058	-0.016	2.6251	0.622
		5	-0.163	-0.182	3.7174	0.591
		6	0.239	0.156	6.1681	0.405
		7	-0.120	-0.071	6.8079	0.449
		8	0.158	0.113	7.9654	0.437

Normality test shows that the error is normally distributed.

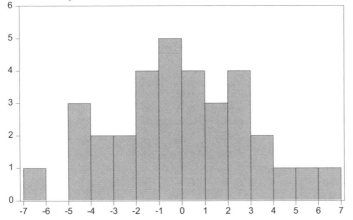

Series: Residuals	
Sample 2 34	
Observations 33	
Mean	2.52e-13
Median	-0.007545
Maximum	6.135892
Minimum	-6.615123
Std. Dev.	2.990935
Skewness	-0.031131
Kurtosis	2.601595
Jarque-Bera	0.223580
Probability	0.894232

There is no serial correlation in residual term according to the below Serial Correlation LM Test

Breusch-Godfrey Serial Correlation LM Test:

F-statistic	1.582359	Prob. F(16,15)	0.1902
Obs*R-squared	20.72253	Prob. Chi-Square(16)	0.1894

As you can see both AR(1) and MA(1) models can be used to model and forecast the given Y variable. Therefore this data series is invertible.

4.5   ARMA model

ARMA model is a combination of two polynomial terms AR and MA, which is used to describe weakly stationary stochastic time series. This model is referred as ARMA (p,q) model. The equation of the model is as below.

p- AR polynomial

q- MA polynomial

A stochastic process (y_t) is said to be a mixture autoregressive moving average model of order 1, ARMA(1,1), if it satisfies the following equation : $Y_t = c + \sum_{i=1}^{p} \emptyset_i Y_{t-i} + \sum_{i=1}^{q} \theta_i \varepsilon_{t-i} + \varepsilon_t$

The properties of an ARMA(1,1)

The properties of the process are a mixture of those of an AR(1) and MA(1) processes .

The (stability) stationarity condition is the one of an AR(1) process (or ARMA(1,0) process) : $|\varphi| < 1$.

The invertibility condition is the one of a MA(1) process (or ARMA(0,1) process) : $|\theta| < 1$.

The representation of an ARMA(1,1) process is fundamental or causal if : $|\varphi| < 1$ and $|\theta| < 1$.

The representation of an ARMA(1,1) process is said to be minimal and causal if : $|\varphi| < 1$, $|\theta| < 1$ and $\varphi \neq \theta$.

Difference between an ARMA model and ARIMA

Simply ARIMA model is the differenced series of ARMA. ARMA model can be created when the given time series are stationary without undergoing any transformation. If the time series variables should be differenced before making them stationary then we use ARIMA model instead of ARMA.

A model with a dth difference to fit and ARMA(p,q) model is called an ARIMA process of order (p,d,q). When additional explanatory variable is involved it is called ARIMAX. SARIMA is the term used for seasonal ARIMA models.

4.6 ARIMA Model

Steps to construct a non seasonal ARIMA model

1. identify if the model is linear or non linear
2. identify if the model is stationary or not
   (Stationary models have horizontally and constantly spread variables.)
3. if the model is not stationary apply the first difference transformation
4. if the model is not stationary after the first difference, then apply the second difference as well.
   (d is the term we use to identify the number of difference we uses in the model, therefore d can be 0,1, or 2. d is simply the difference)
5. if y is the stationary time series then the model will be
   y= constant + weighted sum of last p value of y + weighted sum of last q forecast error

The final model is ARIMA (p,d,q)
Components of non seasonal model is
AR , $\Phi B = 1 - \Phi_1 B - ... - \Phi_p B^P$
MA , $\Theta B = 1 - \theta_1 B - ... - \theta_q B^q$

4.7 Seasonal ARIMA Modeling

Seasonal ARIMA modeling is represented by ARIMA (p,d,q) (P,D,Q) has below structure.

(P,D,Q) is the seasonal term.

P= SAR term or Seasonal Autoregressive term

D= Number of Seasonal Differences

Q= SMA term or Seasonal Moving Average term

We can even mention the seasonal period using a S term at the end of the Seasonal ARIMA model. ARIMA (p,d,q) (P,D,Q)S

Note : First we should identify if seasonal differencing is needed. We shouldn't use more than one seasonal differencing. If we have to use one seasonal differencing then only one or none non-seasonal differencing should be used for the model. Do not use more than two combined non seasonal plus seasonal differences.

Seasonal data can be identified when pure MA or pure AR signature happens at equal time periods.

Seasonal Random Walk Model : ARIMA (0,0,0) (0,1,0)

There is one order of seasonal differencing , one constant term , no other parameters of AR, MA , SAR or SMA. Seasonal difference at period t is y_t - y_{t-12}.

After applying mean to this model it becomes

$\mu = y_t - y_{t-12}$

Seasonal Random Trend Model : ARIMA (0,1,0) (0,1,0)

There is one order of non-seasonal differencing, one order of seasonal differencing and there is no constant or no parameter of AR, MA, SAR or SMA.

Prediction of data

$(\hat{y}_t - y_{t-12})(y_{t-1} - y_{t-13})$

Seasonal Exponential Smoothing Model : ARIMA (0,1,1) (0,1,1)

Trend is smoothed by adding MA (1) and seasonal MA(1)

This model is a common seasonal model.

Example 4.5: ARIMA (PDQ)

Find the ARIMA data sheet in eviews.

This time series is on whole sale potato price of a country from 2003 January to 2010 December. After opening PP data series in e views, click on range. After that you get work structure table. Change its data as shown in the below e-views output. We are going to add 5 more months to the data series, as we are going to use final 5 months for validating data. Therefore start date is 2003M01 and end date is 2011M05.

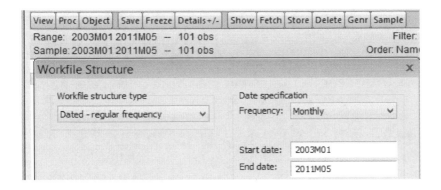

Find the below graph on the distribution of the potato price.

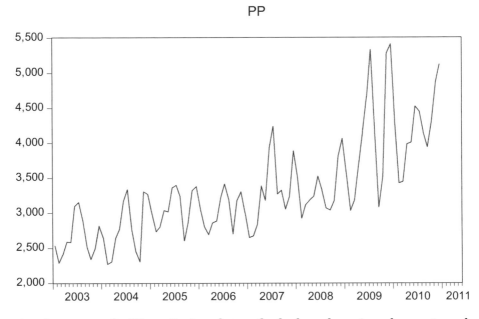

PP

At above graph, Time Series data of whole sale price shows trend and seasonal patterns. It doesn't seems to have a constant variance and constant mean.

Descriptive Statistics	PP
Mean	3121.896
Median	2994.500
Maximum	5410.000
Minimum	1550.000
Std. Dev.	758.8250
Skewness	0.933183
Kurtosis	3.936724

Jarque-Bera	17.44309
Probability	0.000163
Sum	299702.0
Sum Sq. Dev.	54702455
Observations	96

Mean of the data set is Rs3121.89 with standard deviation of Rs.758.86 Maximum whole sale price of potato in is Rs5410.00with the minimum of Rs1550.skewness 0.9331 shows a positive skew in the distribution with kurtosis of 3.93 which indicates the data is not normally distributed. Jarque bera test statistic is also significant (0.0001< 0.05), therefore data set is not normally distributed.

Therefore the data series doesn't seem to be stationary. We can check ACF and PACF to get more idea on data set.

Autocorrelation and Partial Autocorrelation

Sample: 2003M01 2011M05
Included observations: 96

Autocorrelation	Partial Correlation		AC	PAC	Q-Stat	Prob
		1	0.725	0.725	51.999	0.000
		2	0.422	-0.218	69.797	0.000
		3	0.339	0.276	81.428	0.000
		4	0.432	0.255	100.47	0.000
		5	0.594	0.344	136.97	0.000
		6	0.611	0.047	176.04	0.000
		7	0.493	0.047	201.72	0.000
		8	0.346	-0.080	214.55	0.000
		9	0.203	-0.272	218.99	0.000
		10	0.249	0.105	225.79	0.000
		11	0.460	0.264	249.19	0.000
		12	0.527	-0.014	280.34	0.000

Autocorrelation function shows that even more than first three lags are significant and there is a long decay. Therefore it can be identified as a non stationary series. Further it can be seen there is a slight seasonality in ACF model.

When it comes to PACF model first lag is significant and positive where second lags is also significant but negative. 3rd and 4th lags are also significant. It shows there is non stationary data series and the model need to be modified to get correct forecasting.

Dicky Fuller Test

Null Hypothesis: PP has a unit root
Exogenous: Constant
Lag Length: 10 (Automatic - based on SIC, maxlag=11)

		t-Statistic	Prob.*
Augmented Dickey-Fuller test statistic		0.211378	0.9719
Test critical values:	1% level	-3.509281	
	5% level	-2.895924	
	10% level	-2.585172	

*MacKinnon (1996) one-sided p-values.

H_0 : Data Series has a unit root
H_1: Data Set doesn't have unit root
P value (0.9719) =>0.05 , therefore H_0 is not rejected.
Data Series has unit root, therefore it is not stationary.

Making the data set stationary

First difference of the data set is calculated to make the series stationary. Let's check if the first difference adds any changes to stationary dataset.

Sample: 2003M01 2011M05
Included observations: 95

Autocorrelation	Partial Correlation		AC	PAC	Q-Stat	Prob
		1	0.098	0.098	0.9417	0.332
		2	-0.432	-0.446	19.414	0.000
		3	-0.349	-0.307	31.599	0.000
		4	-0.166	-0.428	34.386	0.000
		5	0.237	-0.126	40.146	0.000
		6	0.283	-0.151	48.430	0.000
		7	0.159	0.118	51.091	0.000
		8	-0.015	0.210	51.114	0.000
		9	-0.388	-0.087	67.210	0.000
		10	-0.342	-0.244	79.892	0.000
		11	0.227	0.019	85.552	0.000
		12	0.379	-0.027	101.46	0.000

Above correlogram for the first differenced data shows first spike is positive which a sign of an AR model is. Second and Third Spikes are negatively significant, therefore we can try to fit a MA model as well.(check AC and PAC values).

Differenced PP

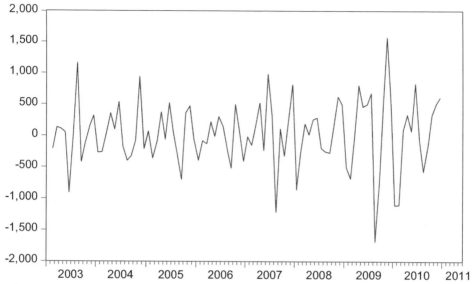

Above graph on differenced PP shows that data has been more stationary.

Testing stationary of differenced data

Null Hypothesis: D(PP) has a unit root			
Exogenous: Constant			
Lag Length: 4 (Automatic - based on SIC, maxlag=11)			
		t-Statistic	Prob.*
Augmented Dickey-Fuller test statistic		-8.176180	0.0000
Test critical values:	1% level	-3.504727	
	5% level	-2.893956	
	10% level	-2.584126	

H_0 : Data Series has a unit root
H_1: Data Set doesn't have unit root
P value =<0.05 , therefore H_0 is rejected.
According to the above table ,Data Series doesn't have unit root, therefore first difference of the series is stationary.

Estimate ARIMA model for whole sale price of potatoes

Accroding to the ACF and PACF models of the first difference we can try to fit both AR and MA models. As first spike is positive let's try AR(1) with MA(2) as the second spike is negatively significant.

Dependent Variable: D(PP,1,12)
Method: Least Squares
Sample (adjusted): 15 96
Included observations: 82 after adjustments
Convergence achieved after 9 iterations
MA Backcast: 13 14

Variable	Coefficient	Std. Error	t-Statistic	Prob.
C	-0.168350	20.74668	-0.008115	0.9935
AR(1)	-0.252785	0.113684	-2.223584	0.0290
MA(2)	-0.448932	0.108433	-4.140191	0.0001

R-squared	0.142856	Mean dependent var	-3.257439
Adjusted R-squared	0.121156	S.D. dependent var	445.0787
S.E. of regression	417.2465	Akaike info criterion	14.94113
Sum squared resid	13753475	Schwarz criterion	15.02918
Log likelihood	-609.5864	Hannan-Quinn criter.	14.97648
F-statistic	6.583263	Durbin-Watson stat	1.974629
Prob(F-statistic)	0.002268		

Inverted AR Roots	-.25	
Inverted MA Roots	.67	-.67

Figure of Fitting ARMA(1,1,0) (0,1,2)^{12} model for whole sale Potato Price

Validating ARMA(1,1,0) (0,1,2)^{12} model : Random Test for Residuals

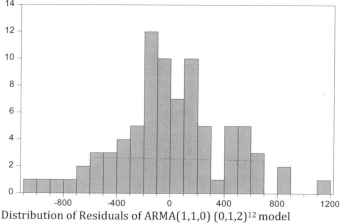

Figure of ACF and PACF of Residuals of ARMA(1,1,0) (0,1,2)^{12} model

Random Test Results shows that the residuals are random. Therefor it validate the terms of "Residuals of a model should be random".

Even the Durbin Watson Test statistic is closer to 2, which proves data are random. Therefor the model has white noise.

Normality Test for Residuals

Series: Residuals	
Sample 15 96	
Observations 82	
Mean	0.403619
Median	-15.89404
Maximum	1158.941
Minimum	-1001.584
Std. Dev.	412.0629
Skewness	0.061653
Kurtosis	3.229564
Jarque-Bera	0.232005
Probability	0.890473

Distribution of Residuals of ARMA(1,1,0) (0,1,2)^{12} model

H_0 : Data are normally distributed

H_1 : Data are not Normally Distributed

78

P-Value of JarqueBeraTest , 0.89 >= 0.05. Therefore H_0 is not rejected. Residuals are normally distributed. It can be identified that the model has Gaussian White Noise.

Therefor ARMA(1,1,0) $(0,1,2)^{12}$ model is valid for future predictions.

Identifying a better model for whole sale price of Potato

When looking at Figure of ACF and PACF graphs, we can see that the third lag is also negatively significant. Therefore we can try to fit an Seasonal MA(3) model as well to see if it is more significant than the ARMA(1,1,0) $(0,1,2)^{12}$ model.

Let's try fitting ARMA(1,1,0) $(0,1,3)^{12}$ for the Data Series.

Dependent Variable: D(PP,1,12)
Method: Least Squares
Sample (adjusted): 15 96
Included observations: 82 after adjustments
Convergence achieved after 347 iterations
MA Backcast: OFF (Roots of MA process too large)

Variable	Coefficient	Std. Error	t-Statistic	Prob.
C	13.14931	0.948459	13.86386	0.0000
AR(1)	-0.577769	0.126740	-4.558691	0.0000
MA(2)	-0.920649	0.140461	-6.554483	0.0000
MA(3)	-0.517670	0.107535	-4.813972	0.0000

R-squared	0.389051	Mean dependent var	-3.257439
Adjusted R-squared	0.365552	S.D. dependent var	445.0787
S.E. of regression	354.5150	Akaike info criterion	14.62693
Sum squared resid	9803110.	Schwarz criterion	14.74433
Log likelihood	-595.7041	Hannan-Quinn criter.	14.67406
F-statistic	16.55671	Durbin-Watson stat	1.943832
Prob(F-statistic)	0.000000		

Inverted AR Roots	-.58		
Inverted MA Roots	1.17	-.58-.32i	-.58+.32i
	Estimated MA process is noninvertible		

Figure of ARMA(1,1,0) $(0,1,3)^{12}$ model for whole sale price of potato- NuwaraEliya

ARMA (1,1,0) $(0,1,3)^{12}$ can also be fitted for above data. Now let's do a validation check for the above model.

Validation of the model ARMA(1,1,0) (0,1,3)^{12}
Random Test for the residual of ARMA(1,1,0) (0,1,3)^{12} Model

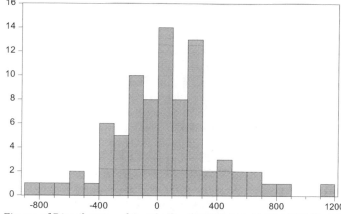

Figure of ACF and PACF for the residuals of ARMA(1,1,0) (0,1,3)^{12}

Above figure shows that residuals are random. Even the test statistic of Durbin Watson test is 1.94 which is closer to 2, which means residuals are random. Therefore there is white noise.

Normality Test for the residuals of ARMA(1,1,0) (0,1,3)^{12} Model

Series: Residuals	
Sample 15 96	
Observations 82	
Mean	38.79390
Median	53.19525
Maximum	1155.362
Minimum	-865.7682
Std. Dev.	345.6913
Skewness	0.269641
Kurtosis	4.003942
Jarque-Bera	4.437307
Probability	0.108755

Figure of Distribution of Residuals of ARMA(1,1,0) (0,1,3)^{12} Model

H_0 : Data are normally distributed

H_1 : Data are not Normally Distributed

P-Value of JarqueBeraTest 1.087>= 0.05. Therefore H_0 is not rejected. Residuals are normally distributed. It can be identified that the model has Gaussian White Noise.

Forecasting
Data can be forecasted using ARMA(1,1,0) $(0,1,2)^{12}$ model. Therefore it is selected as the most suitable model for the Time Series Data of Whole Sale Price of Potato

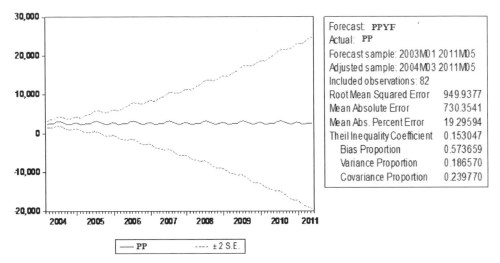

Forecast: PPYF	
Actual: PP	
Forecast sample: 2003M01 2011M05	
Adjusted sample: 2004M03 2011M05	
Included observations: 82	
Root Mean Squared Error	949.9377
Mean Absolute Error	730.3541
Mean Abs. Percent Error	19.29594
Theil Inequality Coefficient	0.153047
Bias Proportion	0.573659
Variance Proportion	0.186570
Covariance Proportion	0.239770

Forecasting of ARMA(1,1,0) $(0,1,2)^{12}$ model

Whole sale price of Potato for next Five months can be forecasted as below with 95% of confidence. It may vary with in Standard Deviation of 949.9377 (Check the statistics of above figure)

Example 4.6 : ARIMA
Find the data set in excel sheet named as CPI
First let's draw the time series plot for the CPI.
Figure shows the temporal variability of the monthly series of Colombo Price Index. Figure of Temporal Variability of CP index indicates that CP index has been increasing over time and it confirms data series is not stationary. There is a trend in data series.

Figure of Temporal Variability of CP index

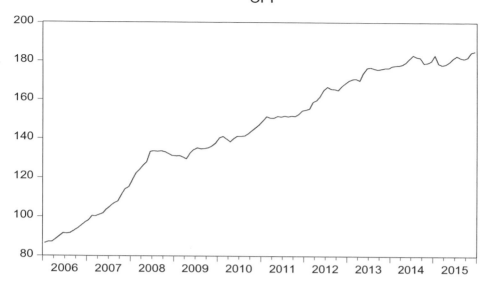

CPI

Figure of Distribution of CPI series and basic descriptive statistics

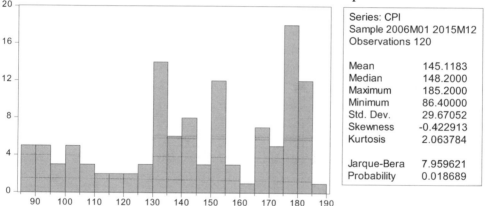

Series: CPI	
Sample 2006M01 2015M12	
Observations 120	
Mean	145.1183
Median	148.2000
Maximum	185.2000
Minimum	86.40000
Std. Dev.	29.67052
Skewness	-0.422913
Kurtosis	2.063784
Jarque-Bera	7.959621
Probability	0.018689

Figure of Distribution of CPI series and basic descriptive statistics shows the basic descriptive statistics of the CPI time series. Fig2 indicates that monthly CPI varies from 864 min to 185.2 max with a means of 145.1. The J-B Statistic (JB Statistics 7.9, p value 0.01) indicates that the distribution of the CPI IS significantly deviate from the normality.(H0: data are normally distributed). CPI series is not normally distributed.

Correlogram of CPI

Autocorrelation	Partial Correlation		AC	PAC	Q-Stat	Prob
		1	0.974	0.974	116.82	0.000
		2	0.948	-0.029	228.33	0.000
		3	0.922	-0.010	334.67	0.000
		4	0.896	-0.007	436.00	0.000
		5	0.870	-0.022	532.30	0.000
		6	0.843	-0.023	623.57	0.000
		7	0.816	-0.028	709.75	0.000
		8	0.788	-0.014	790.98	0.000
		9	0.761	-0.006	867.45	0.000
		10	0.735	-0.000	939.41	0.000
		11	0.709	-0.013	1007.0	0.000
		12	0.681	-0.051	1069.9	0.000
		13	0.654	-0.002	1128.5	0.000
		14	0.628	0.000	1183.0	0.000
		15	0.601	-0.030	1233.4	0.000
		16	0.573	-0.039	1279.6	0.000
		17	0.544	-0.028	1321.8	0.000
		18	0.516	-0.017	1359.9	0.000
		19	0.488	-0.007	1394.4	0.000
		20	0.460	-0.009	1425.5	0.000
		21	0.433	-0.012	1453.3	0.000
		22	0.408	0.021	1478.2	0.000
		23	0.385	0.011	1500.5	0.000
		24	0.361	-0.016	1520.4	0.000
		25	0.339	0.011	1538.1	0.000
		26	0.318	0.009	1553.8	0.000
		27	0.298	0.002	1567.9	0.000
		28	0.280	0.007	1580.3	0.000
		29	0.261	-0.013	1591.3	0.000
		30	0.245	0.026	1601.0	0.000
		31	0.228	-0.026	1609.6	0.000
		32	0.211	-0.008	1617.0	0.000
		33	0.196	0.007	1623.5	0.000
		34	0.180	-0.032	1628.9	0.000

Correlogram of CPI indicates that the autocorrelation are decreasing with the increase of lag and also most of those are significant from zero. This reveals original series is non stationary. This was confirmed by d-f test and corresponding results are shown in below table.

Null Hypothesis: CPI has a unit root			
Exogenous: Constant			
Lag Length: 1 (Automatic - based on SIC, maxlag=12)			
		t-Statistic	Prob.*
Augmented Dickey-Fuller test statistic		-2.007397	0.2834
Test critical values:	1% level	-3.486551	
	5% level	-2.886074	
	10% level	-2.579931	
*MacKinnon (1996) one-sided p-values.			

Null hypothesis is not rejected. (Null hypothesis is indicated in the table) CPI series has a unit root.

Now let's check the first difference.

		t-Statistic	Prob.*
Null Hypothesis: D(CPI) has a unit root			
Exogenous: Constant			
Lag Length: 0 (Automatic - based on SIC, maxlag=12)			
Augmented Dickey-Fuller test statistic		-7.980614	0.0000
Test critical values:	1% level	-3.486551	
	5% level	-2.886074	
	10% level	-2.579931	
*MacKinnon (1996) one-sided p-values.			

The first difference does not show any unit root .therefore data series is stationary. Now let's identify a suitable model using correlogram. Below is the correlogram for the first difference of the CIP series.

Autocorrelation	Partial Correlation		AC	PAC	Q-Stat	Prob
		1	0.291	0.291	10.316	0.001
		2	0.023	-0.067	10.382	0.006
		3	-0.046	-0.037	10.643	0.014
		4	0.150	0.194	13.463	0.009
		5	0.119	0.018	15.248	0.009
		6	0.151	0.122	18.172	0.006
		7	0.022	-0.036	18.232	0.011
		8	-0.040	-0.057	18.436	0.018
		9	-0.287	-0.301	29.205	0.001
		10	-0.139	-0.026	31.754	0.000
		11	0.095	0.146	32.961	0.001
		12	0.201	0.127	38.422	0.000
		13	0.013	0.028	38.447	0.000
		14	-0.031	0.061	38.576	0.000
		15	-0.107	-0.083	40.153	0.000
		16	0.028	0.009	40.261	0.001
		17	0.012	-0.086	40.281	0.001
		18	0.119	0.015	42.293	0.001
		19	0.121	0.093	44.395	0.001
		20	-0.053	-0.067	44.798	0.001
		21	-0.264	-0.132	55.049	0.000
		22	-0.152	-0.068	58.458	0.000
		23	-0.042	-0.067	58.727	0.000
		24	0.107	0.079	60.452	0.000
		25	0.004	0.034	60.455	0.000
		26	-0.130	-0.070	63.069	0.000
		27	-0.177	-0.027	67.966	0.000
		28	0.011	0.136	67.986	0.000
		29	0.056	-0.003	68.483	0.000
		30	0.157	0.004	72.483	0.000

Identification of models for the mean equation

Based on the correlogram of the first difference, the following models were selected for the mean equation.

It can be seen that the autocorrelation at lag 1,9,12 and 21 are significantly different from zero. But the partial autocorrelation only 1 and 9 are significantly different from zero. we do not consider MA parts for the mean equation.

The following AR models were considered for the mean equation of ARIMA (1, 1, 0) *(1, 0, 0)^{12}.

$$y_t = \emptyset_1 y_{t-1} + \emptyset_9 y_{t-9} + \emptyset_{12} y_{t-12}$$

AR(1) model

Dependent Variable: D(CPI)
Method: Least Squares
Sample (adjusted): 2006M03 2015M12
Included observations: 118 after adjustments
Convergence achieved after 3 iterations

Variable	Coefficient	Std. Error	t-Statistic	Prob.
C	0.830661	0.170947	4.859182	0.0000
AR(1)	0.290900	0.088853	3.273949	0.0014

R-squared	0.084587	Mean dependent var	0.831356
Adjusted R-squared	0.076695	S.D. dependent var	1.370364
S.E. of regression	1.316765	Akaike info criterion	3.405038
Sum squared resid	201.1291	Schwarz criterion	3.451998
Log likelihood	-198.8972	Hannan-Quinn criter.	3.424105
F-statistic	10.71874	Durbin-Watson stat	1.954846
Prob(F-statistic)	0.001398		

Inverted AR Roots	.29

AR(1) AR(9) model

Dependent Variable: D(CPI) Method: Least Squares
Sample (adjusted): 2006M11 2015M12
Included observations: 110 after adjustments
Convergence achieved after 2 iterations

Variable	Coefficient	Std. Error	t-Statistic	Prob.
C	0.827704	0.123025	6.727962	0.0000
AR(1)	0.281978	0.088300	3.193413	0.0018
AR(9)	-0.287908	0.089594	-3.213487	0.0017

R-squared	0.166757	Mean dependent var	0.828182
Adjusted R-squared	0.151183	S.D. dependent var	1.408762
S.E. of regression	1.297911	Akaike info criterion	3.386283
Sum squared resid	180.2493	Schwarz criterion	3.459932
Log likelihood	-183.2456	Hannan-Quinn criter.	3.416156
F-statistic	10.70697	Durbin-Watson stat	1.945008
Prob(F-statistic)	0.000058		

Inverted AR Roots	.85+.30i	.85-.30i	.47+.75i	.47-.75i
	-.12+.85i	-.12-.85i	-.64+.56i	-.64-.56i
	-.84			

AR(1) AR(9)AR(12) model ,E views equation: d(cpi,1)c ar(1) ar(9) ar(12)

Dependent Variable: D(CPI,1)
Method: Least Squares
Sample (adjusted): 2007M02 2015M12
Included observations: 107 after adjustments
Convergence achieved after 3 iterations

Variable	Coefficient	Std. Error	t-Statistic	Prob.
C	0.802791	0.153985	5.213436	0.0000
AR(1)	0.257364	0.088523	2.907315	0.0045
AR(9)	-0.288496	0.089254	-3.232291	0.0016
AR(12)	0.219512	0.097773	2.245121	0.0269

R-squared	0.203950	Mean dependent var	0.813084
Adjusted R-squared	0.180764	S.D. dependent var	1.425448
S.E. of regression	1.290197	Akaike info criterion	3.384133
Sum squared resid	171.4546	Schwarz criterion	3.484052
Log likelihood	-177.0511	Hannan-Quinn criter.	3.424639
F-statistic	8.796289	Durbin-Watson stat	1.946772
Prob(F-statistic)	0.000030		

Inverted AR Roots	.83+.38i	.83-.38i	.82	.49+.81i
	.49-.81i	-.04-.89i	-.04+.89i	-.39-.69i
	-.39+.69i	-.72+.50i	-.72-.50i	-.91

Three models we checked are
I.   AR(1)
II.   AR(1) AR(9)
III. AR(1) AR(9) AR(12)

There isn't any seasonal pattern and there isn't any seasonal pattern

Comparison of Postulated Models.

The 3 possible models identified for the mean equation was compared in the below table. These possible models are called postulate models. The model with less AIC value is selected as the best suited model for the CPI time series.

Table of comparison of difference statistics of the 3 postulated models.

| Model | Sig of the parameters | | | | Inferential Stat | | |
	Constant	AR (1)	AR (9)	AR (12)	AIC	SC	HQC
I	Sig	Sig	-	-	3.405038	3.451998	3.424105
II	Sig	Sig	Sig	-	3.386283	3.459932	3.416156
III	Sig	Sig	Sig	Sig	3.384133	3.484052	3.424639

Results in Table of comparison of difference statistics of the 3 postulated models indicate that all parameters in the 3 models are significant. However the information statistics are the lowest in the model 3 which has AR(1) AND ar(9) parameters. This indicates that the present value of CPI has a significant impact from the immediate past value. As well as values of 9th month prior this phenomena is not easy to interpret from the practical point of view.

As the next level we have to conduct Diagnostic Test for Residuals for for the best model. We can select model II as the best fitted model, because it has the best information criteria.

Example 4.7: Seasonal ARIMA

Find the dataset in Excel sheet which is named as Sales Price. Time Series Analysis for Sales Price for strawberry in town A.

Histogram of Strawberry Sales Price

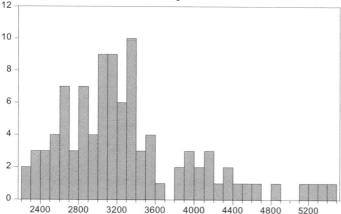

Series: SALES_PRICE	
Sample 1 96	
Observations 96	
Mean	3305.018
Median	3180.690
Maximum	5409.530
Minimum	2269.580
Std. Dev.	705.1734
Skewness	1.073168
Kurtosis	3.929148
Jarque-Bera	21.88031
Probability	0.000018

Above histogram is of strawberry sales prices in town A. The sales price of strawberry varies between Rs.2270 (min=2269.58) and Rs.5410 (max=5409.53). The average sales price is Rs.3305 (mean=3305.018) and standard deviation is 705.17. The sale piece of potato is positively skewed (skew= 1.073). According to the Jarque-Bera test p-value is significant. It means the sales are not normal.

Time series plot of strawberry Sale Price

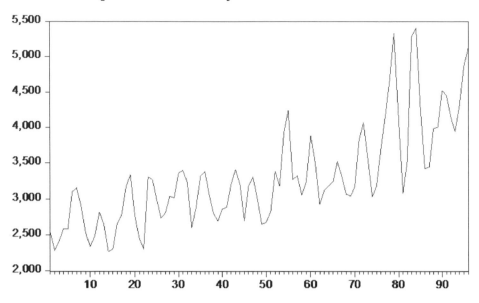

Above plot shows time series plot of strawberry sale price in town A from 2003 to 2010. According to the figure it can identified the trend as well as a seasonal variation and it has an upward trend. It shows the growth of the sale price over the period. There for it can be concluded that the time series is non stationary.

Dickey-Fuller test for Original Sale Price

Null Hypothesis: SALES_PRICE has a unit root		
Exogenous: Constant		
Lag Length: 10 (Automatic - based on SIC, maxlag=11)		
	t-Statistic	Prob.*
Augmented Dickey-Fuller test statistic	0.211378	0.9719

According to the Augmented Dickey-Fuller test, the test statistics is not significant (p-value=0.9719). It can be concluded with 95% confidence that the observed sales price is non stationary. Then it suggests getting a fist difference of the series.

ACF of the Observed Series

Sample: 1 96
Included observations: 96

Autocorrelation	Partial Correlation		AC	PAC	Q-Stat	Prob
		1	0.754	0.754	56.363	0.000
		2	0.440	-0.301	75.698	0.000
		3	0.348	0.366	87.943	0.000
		4	0.455	0.262	109.09	0.000
		5	0.577	0.192	143.48	0.000
		6	0.594	0.136	180.41	0.000
		7	0.503	0.016	207.16	0.000
		8	0.367	-0.090	221.58	0.000
		9	0.244	-0.197	228.03	0.000
		10	0.289	0.204	237.19	0.000
		11	0.490	0.270	263.78	0.000
		12	0.557	-0.120	298.50	0.000
		13	0.382	-0.155	315.00	0.000
		14	0.164	-0.074	318.09	0.000
		15	0.124	0.019	319.88	0.000
		16	0.226	-0.069	325.91	0.000
		17	0.306	-0.035	337.08	0.000
		18	0.281	-0.040	346.57	0.000
		19	0.216	0.079	352.26	0.000
		20	0.093	-0.134	353.34	0.000
		21	0.002	-0.005	353.34	0.000
		22	0.057	0.035	353.75	0.000
		23	0.204	0.030	359.10	0.000
		24	0.257	0.063	367.76	0.000
		25	0.151	0.060	370.78	0.000
		26	0.005	-0.015	370.78	0.000
		27	-0.019	-0.038	370.83	0.000
		28	0.049	-0.038	371.16	0.000

Correlogram indicates that the autocorrelation at first all lags are significantly different form zero. Thus it can be concluded that the observed series is non stationary. This suggests the series has to make stationary to decide ARIMA model.

Dickey-Fuller test for first difference series of Sale Price

Null Hypothesis: D(SALES_PRICE) has a unit root		
Exogenous: Constant		
Lag Length: 4 (Automatic - based on SIC, maxlag=11)		
	t-Statistic	Prob.*
Augmented Dickey-Fuller test statistic	-8.176180	0.0000

According to the results of Augmented Dickey-Fuller test for the first difference (table 1.2), confirms the series is stationary. The Dickey-Fuller test statistics is significant (p-value=0.000). It can be concluded with 95% confidence that the observed sales price is stationary. In order to identify the stationary of the first difference series the ACF and PACF was obtained.

ACF and PACF of first difference series of sale price

Sample: 1 96
Included observations: 95

Autocorrelation	Partial Correlation		AC	PAC	Q-Stat	Prob
		1	0.181	0.181	3.2247	0.073
		2	-0.493	-0.544	27.318	0.000
		3	-0.448	-0.311	47.454	0.000
		4	-0.060	-0.291	47.817	0.000
		5	0.246	-0.180	54.027	0.000
		6	0.262	-0.092	61.119	0.000
		7	0.146	0.127	63.343	0.000
		8	-0.047	0.174	63.573	0.000
		9	-0.371	-0.165	78.360	0.000
		10	-0.376	-0.317	93.695	0.000
		11	0.257	0.106	100.93	0.000
		12	0.478	-0.044	126.32	0.000
		13	0.097	-0.077	127.37	0.000
		14	-0.273	-0.005	135.82	0.000
		15	-0.293	-0.027	145.69	0.000
		16	-0.044	-0.066	145.92	0.000
		17	0.159	-0.020	148.92	0.000
		18	0.164	-0.061	152.16	0.000
		19	0.164	0.030	155.41	0.000
		20	-0.047	-0.052	155.68	0.000
		21	-0.321	-0.028	168.48	0.000
		22	-0.171	-0.004	172.18	0.000
		23	0.175	-0.044	176.12	0.000
		24	0.333	0.098	190.52	0.000
		25	0.106	0.071	192.02	0.000
		26	-0.236	-0.026	199.44	0.000

The correlogram shows ACF and PACF of the first difference series of strabeery sale price. According to the figure, lag 1, lag 12 and etc significantly different from zero. There for it can be identified that the series has sesonal variation futher. Then it should be getting the long term seasonal difference of the first difference series.

ACF and PACF of first and seasonal difference for the seris of sale price

Sample: 1 96
Included observations: 83

Autocorrelation	Partial Correlation		AC	PAC	Q-Stat	Prob
		1	-0.090	-0.090	0.6906	0.406
		2	-0.283	-0.293	7.6616	0.022
		3	-0.122	-0.200	8.9730	0.030
		4	-0.036	-0.189	9.0874	0.059
		5	0.086	-0.060	9.7555	0.082
		6	0.069	-0.023	10.188	0.117
		7	-0.165	-0.205	12.726	0.079
		8	0.079	0.037	13.310	0.102
		9	0.139	0.086	15.164	0.087
		10	0.006	0.061	15.168	0.126
		11	0.126	0.267	16.727	0.116
		12	-0.457	-0.391	37.479	0.000
		13	-0.076	-0.074	38.054	0.000
		14	0.227	-0.061	43.328	0.000
		15	0.011	-0.189	43.341	0.000
		16	-0.039	-0.106	43.501	0.000
		17	0.009	-0.131	43.509	0.000
		18	0.020	0.076	43.554	0.001
		19	0.079	-0.066	44.239	0.001
		20	-0.084	-0.075	45.027	0.001
		21	-0.218	-0.116	50.440	0.000
		22	0.138	0.011	52.651	0.000
		23	0.145	0.271	55.127	0.000
		24	-0.021	-0.235	55.181	0.000
		25	0.042	0.092	55.399	0.000
		26	-0.098	-0.019	56.599	0.000
		27	-0.006	-0.070	56.604	0.001
		28	0.080	0.023	57.418	0.001
		29	0.049	-0.000	57.733	0.001
		30	-0.163	-0.033	61.290	0.001
		31	0.005	-0.047	61.294	0.001
		32	0.041	-0.033	61.528	0.001
		33	0.177	0.020	65.942	0.001
		34	-0.009	0.021	65.954	0.001

According to the above figure it can be concluded the first difference and seasonal difference is stationary. The stationary of the series also confirmed by the Dickey-Fuller test (Appendix 01). The Dickey-Fuller test statistic is significant (p-value=0.000). It can be concluded with 95% confidence that the observed series is stationary.

Identification of ARIMA Model

In order to identify the suitable ARIMA models, the ACF was obtained in ACF and PACF of first and seasonal difference for the seris of sale price . According to the above ACF and PACF it can be assumed that the series would have come from AR(1),AR(2),AR(3),SAR(12), MA(1),SMA(12). In order to compare the possible models, comparison of the following statistics and future diagnostics were done (table of Comparison of significance of the parameters).

According to the below table clearly confirms that the constant term is not significant in model 2 [AR (1), MA (1)](Appendix 03),model 3[SAR (12), MA (1)](Appendix 04) and the model 4 [AR (2), SMA (12)](Appendix 05).The constant of the first model significant [AR (1), SAR (12), MA (1)] (Appendix 02). Therefore the below models can be claimed that the model 2, model 3 and model 4 are not suitable for the observed series.

Table of Comparison of significance of the parameters

Model	Sig. of the parameters	MSE	D.W. Statistics	Akaike info criterion	Schwarz criterion	Hannan-Quinn criter
Constant AR(1) SAR(12) MA(1)	Sig Sig Sig Sig	101384	1.833360	14.53851	14.66699	14.58954
Constant AR(1) MA(1)	Not Sig. Sig Sig	162371	1.820286	14.87693	14.96498	14.91228
Constant SAR(12) MA(1)	Not Sig Sig Sig	116415	1.374699	14.69202	14.78763	14.73004
Constant AR(2) SMA(12)	Not Sig Sig Sig	94006	2.262391	14.30507	14.39375	14.34065

According to the results above table, it indicates that the information criteria are much smaller for 4th model [AR (2), SMA (12)]. Also it can be seen that Mean square error (MSE) is also lower in 4th model

(94006) compared with other models. According to the these results it can be concluded that the best model is AR(2) and SMA(12) model. Under these assumptions there are mainly two models

Residual Diagnostics for the Model

After select the best model, it should be checked validity of the model. It can be checked by residual diagnostics.

The Q-statistic is often used as a test of whether the series is white noise. There remains the practical problem of choosing the order of lag to use for the test. If you choose too small a lag, the test may not detect serial correlation at high-order lags. However, if you choose too large a lag, the test may have low power since the significant correlation at one lag may be diluted by insignificant correlations at other lags.

Figure of Q statistics of Model

Sample: 1 96
Included observations: 81
Q-statistic probabilities adjusted for 2 ARMA terms

Autocorrelation	Partial Correlation		AC	PAC	Q-Stat	Prob
		1	-0.136	-0.136	1.5454	
		2	-0.059	-0.079	1.8446	
		3	-0.213	-0.239	6.7718	0.016
		4	-0.123	-0.214	7.0839	0.029
		5	0.035	-0.076	7.1921	0.066
		6	0.178	0.094	10.030	0.040
		7	-0.098	-0.140	10.903	0.053
		8	0.046	-0.000	11.102	0.085
		9	0.003	0.065	11.103	0.134
		10	-0.193	-0.210	14.637	0.067
		11	0.175	0.107	17.571	0.040
		12	-0.156	-0.169	19.937	0.030
		13	-0.064	-0.185	20.342	0.041
		14	0.087	0.004	21.097	0.049
		15	-0.066	-0.161	21.537	0.063
		16	-0.035	-0.155	21.663	0.086
		17	0.051	-0.123	21.937	0.109
		18	-0.016	-0.029	21.966	0.144
		19	0.045	-0.077	22.187	0.178
		20	0.028	-0.122	22.271	0.220
		21	-0.120	-0.087	23.882	0.201
		22	0.064	-0.124	24.341	0.228
		23	0.108	0.049	25.687	0.219
		24	-0.099	-0.177	26.844	0.217
		25	0.118	-0.060	28.520	0.197
		26	-0.009	0.021	28.530	0.238
		27	0.050	0.026	28.838	0.271
		28	0.013	-0.023	28.861	0.317
		29	0.051	0.095	29.203	0.351
		30	-0.207	-0.140	34.844	0.174
		31	0.050	-0.060	35.186	0.198
		32	-0.018	0.031	35.229	0.234
		33	0.128	0.071	37.522	0.195
		34	0.026	-0.045	37.617	0.228

H_0: Q statistics is not significant
H_1: Q statistics is significant

According to the figure of Q statistics of model ,H₀is accepted. All residuals are in the significant level. Therefore it can be concluded with 95% confidence that the Q statistic is significant.

Normality Test

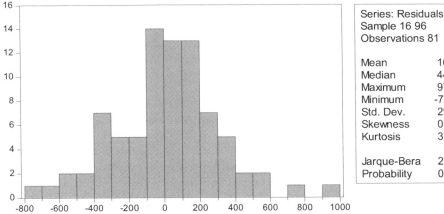

H₀: Errors are normal

H₁: Errors are not normal

According to the normality test ,p-value is 0.2374 when the Jarque-Bera value is 2.8758. Therefore H₀ is accepted. It can be concluded with95% confidence that the errors are normally distributed.

Serial Correlation LM Test

Breusch-Godfrey Serial Correlation LM Test:				
F-statistic	1.559462	Prob. F(8,70)		0.1530
Obs*R-squared	12.04660	Prob. Chi-Square(8)		0.1491
Variable	Coefficient	Std. Error	t-Statistic	Prob.
C	-0.600239	12.24805	-0.049007	0.9611
AR(2)	0.104189	0.323252	0.322316	0.7482
MA(12)	0.012289	0.036988	0.332246	0.7407
RESID(-1)	-0.214384	0.120954	-1.772449	0.0807
RESID(-2)	-0.239591	0.335218	-0.714732	0.4772
RESID(-3)	-0.286289	0.122871	-2.329994	0.0227
RESID(-4)	-0.215881	0.160376	-1.346091	0.1826
RESID(-5)	-0.070647	0.128933	-0.547933	0.5855
RESID(-6)	0.066784	0.125776	0.530978	0.5971
RESID(-7)	-0.136742	0.122858	-1.113008	0.2695
RESID(-8)	0.010918	0.121468	0.089885	0.9286
R-squared	0.148723	Mean dependent var		16.27466
Adjusted R-squared	0.027112	S.D. dependent var		299.2486

S.E. of regression	295.1640	Akaike info criterion	14.33859
Sum squared resid	6098525.	Schwarz criterion	14.66376
Log likelihood	-569.7129	Hannan-Quinn criter.	14.46905
F-statistic	1.222944	Durbin-Watson stat	1.987874
Prob(F-statistic)	0.291941		

H_0: Residuals have constant variance
H_1: Residuals have not constant variance

According to the serial correlation LM test, the residuals are not significant differ from zero. Therefore H_0 is accepted at 5% significant level. It can be concluded with 95% confidence that the residuals have constant variance.

According to these results it can be concluded that the best model is MA (2) and SMA (12) model. It has minimum residuals sums of square value than others and all assumptions proved. Then research can recommend MA (2) and SMA (12) model is suitable for the estimate strawberry sale price

The final Model is;
$$y_t = -0.016537 + u_t$$
$$y_t - y_{t-1} = -0.0165 + (1 + 0.9677B^2)(1 + 0.869\ B^{12})e_t$$

Appendix
Appendix 01:

Null Hypothesis: X has a unit root
Exogenous: Constant
Lag Length: 1 (Automatic - based on SIC, maxlag=11)

		t-Statistic	Prob.*
Augmented Dickey-Fuller test statistic		-8.851444	0.0000
Test critical values:	1% level	-3.513344	
	5% level	-2.897678	
	10% level	-2.586103	

*MacKinnon (1996) one-sided p-values.

Augmented Dickey-Fuller Test Equation
Dependent Variable: D(X)
Method: Least Squares
Sample (adjusted): 16 96
Included observations: 81 after adjustments

Variable	Coefficient	Std. Error	t-Statistic	Prob.
X(-1)	-1.437011	0.162348	-8.851444	0.0000
D(X(-1))	0.321094	0.112812	2.846268	0.0056
C	-0.149613	47.76976	-0.003132	0.9975

R-squared	0.587828	Mean dependent var	2.753457
Adjusted R-squared	0.577259	S.D. dependent var	661.0855
S.E. of regression	429.8280	Akaike info criterion	15.00098
Sum squared resid	14410664	Schwarz criterion	15.08966
Log likelihood	-604.5397	Hannan-Quinn criter.	15.03656
F-statistic	55.62064	Durbin-Watson stat	2.127961
Prob(F-statistic)	0.000000		

Appendix 02:

Dependent Variable: D(SALES_PRICE,1,12)
Method: Least Squares
Sample (adjusted): 27 96
Included observations: 70 after adjustments
Failure to improve SSR after 24 iterations
MA Backcast: 26

Variable	Coefficient	Std. Error	t-Statistic	Prob.
C	4.646708	1.980399	2.346349	0.0220
AR(1)	0.454000	0.117880	3.851367	0.0003
SAR(12)	-0.673009	0.104781	-6.422997	0.0000
MA(1)	-0.999938	0.062585	-15.97727	0.0000

R-squared	0.496708	Mean dependent var	-10.72043
Adjusted R-squared	0.473831	S.D. dependent var	465.7546
S.E. of regression	337.8469	Akaike info criterion	14.53851
Sum squared resid	7533273.	Schwarz criterion	14.66699
Log likelihood	-504.8478	Hannan-Quinn criter.	14.58954
F-statistic	21.71217	Durbin-Watson stat	1.833360
Prob(F-statistic)	0.000000		

Inverted AR Roots	.93-.25i	.93+.25i	.68-.68i	.68+.68i
	.45	.25+.93i	.25-.93i	-.25+.93i
	-.25-.93i	-.68+.68i	-.68+.68i	-.93-.25i
	-.93+.25i			
Inverted MA Roots	1.00			

Appendix 03:

Dependent Variable: D(SALES_PRICE,1,12)				
Method: Least Squares				
Sample (adjusted): 15 96				
Included observations: 82 after adjustments				
Convergence achieved after 26 iterations				
MA Backcast: 14				

Variable	Coefficient	Std. Error	t-Statistic	Prob.
C	1.367632	4.742250	0.288393	0.7738
AR(1)	0.579553	0.099420	5.829341	0.0000
MA(1)	-0.983771	0.018413	-53.42910	0.0000

R-squared	0.196160	Mean dependent var	-3.257439
Adjusted R-squared	0.175809	S.D. dependent var	445.0787
S.E. of regression	404.0644	Akaike info criterion	14.87693
Sum squared resid	12898177	Schwarz criterion	14.96498
Log likelihood	-606.9539	Hannan-Quinn criter.	14.91228
F-statistic	9.639117	Durbin-Watson stat	1.820286
Prob(F-statistic)	0.000180		

Inverted AR Roots	.58
Inverted MA Roots	.98

Appendix 04:

Dependent Variable: D(SALES_PRICE,1,12)				
Method: Least Squares				
Sample (adjusted): 26 96				
Included observations: 71 after adjustments				
Convergence achieved after 14 iterations				
MA Backcast: 25				

Variable	Coefficient	Std. Error	t-Statistic	Prob.
C	3.829135	4.571036	0.837695	0.4051
AR(12)	-0.774895	0.103109	-7.515312	0.0000
MA(1)	-0.829098	0.066560	-12.45641	0.0000

R-squared	0.387491	Mean dependent var	-8.912535
Adjusted R-squared	0.369476	S.D. dependent var	462.6667
S.E. of regression	367.3829	Akaike info criterion	14.69202
Sum squared resid	9177975.	Schwarz criterion	14.78763
Log likelihood	-518.5668	Hannan-Quinn criter.	14.73004
F-statistic	21.50940	Durbin-Watson stat	1.374699
Prob(F-statistic)	0.000000		

Inverted AR Roots	.95+.25i	.95-.25i	.69-.69i	.69-.69i
	.25-.95i	.25+.95i	-.25+.95i	-.25-.95i
	-.69-.69i	-.69+.69i	-.95+.25i	-.95-.25i
Inverted MA Roots	.83			

Appendix 05:

Dependent Variable: D(SALES_PRICE,1,12)
Method: Least Squares
Sample (adjusted): 16 96
Included observations: 81 after adjustments
Convergence achieved after 12 iterations
MA Backcast: 4 15

Variable	Coefficient	Std. Error	t-Statistic	Prob.
C	5.050947	12.57373	0.401706	0.6890
AR(2)	-0.344869	0.105839	-3.258435	0.0017
MA(12)	-0.886671	0.036924	-24.01326	0.0000

R-squared	0.551986	Mean dependent var	-2.208519
Adjusted R-squared	0.540498	S.D. dependent var	447.7498
S.E. of regression	303.5143	Akaike info criterion	14.30507
Sum squared resid	7185431.	Schwarz criterion	14.39375
Log likelihood	-576.3553	Hannan-Quinn criter.	14.34065
F-statistic	48.05076	Durbin-Watson stat	2.262391
Prob(F-statistic)	0.000000		

Inverted AR Roots	-.00+.59i	-.00-.59i		
Inverted MA Roots	.99	.86+.50i	.86-.50i	.50-.86i
	.50+.86i	.00-.99i	-.00+.99i	-.50-.86i
	-.50+.86i	-.86-.50i	-.86+.50i	-.99

Chapter Five: ARCH/GARCH

5.1 Introduction

ARCH model is used to model conditional variance that depends on time. GARCH is the generalized autoregression conditional heteroskedastic model. ARCH and GARCH models are used to measure the volatility of financial time series. When there is heteroskedasticity present in a model there is ARCH effect. We can test ARCH effect using Lagrange multiplier test or Ljung box statistic.

In other words, Autoregressive conditional hetertoskedasticity are used for the time series with differencing variance. Differencing variance or heteroskedasticity can mostly be identified in financial time series.

The basic version of the least squares model assumes that, the expected value of all error terms when squared is the same at any given point. This assumption is called homoskedasticity of error term. ARCH/GARCH models can be identified as time series models for heteroskedasticity. In regression modeling and time series modeling it is generally assumed that distribution of e_t is serially uncorrelated. But

Most of the financial time series errors are serially correlated. That means residuals are not normally distributed. This phenomenon can be illustrated as below picture. The residual term of the variables involved in ARCH/GARCH models usually looks as the below picture if taken into a scatter diagram.

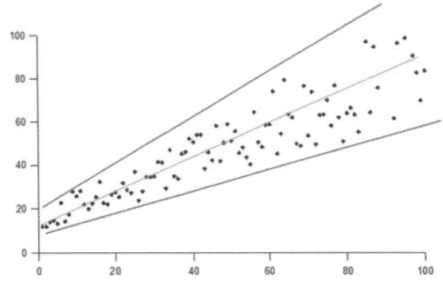

The existence of serial autocorrelation in error term violates the standard assumptions in ARIMA.

Ignoring the assumption on serial correlation gives below results

1. Estimates are no longer efficient
2. Standard errors are not valid
3. Estimate are biased and inconsistent
4. Forecast value are inefficient

Therefore we should use a separate model to which is able to capture this characteristic of error term.

5.2   Parsimonious Models

When we calculate models with many variables, we meet over parameterized models. These models are the models with many lags of a variable, many regressors or both many lags of a variable and many regressors. Few or many of these lags or regressors can be with insignificant coefficients due to multicolinearity issue. Therefore removing these variables or lags makes the model more efficient and easy to use. The newly modified model with reduced insignificant variables or lags is called Parsimonious Models.

Redundant variable test is used in this study to identify remove insignificant coefficients from the model.

101

5.3 ARCH Model

In an standard linear regression of an Ordinary Least square method $(y_i = \alpha + \beta x_t + e_i)$ the residuals (e_i) are constant. When residuals are not constant we used weighted least square to estimate regression coefficient

Where x_t is residuals of return ARCH(1) model equation is
The ARCH(1) model for the variance of model x_t is that conditional on x_{t-1}, the variance at time t is Var (Var X$_t$| Var X$_{t-1}$) = σ_t^2 = α_0 + $\alpha_1 x_{t-1}^2$

Conditions for the equation to be stationary
The parameters α_0 and α_1 should be positive and α_1 should be less than 1. In most financial time series, condition of normality of residuals are not that considered. When x_t is stationary process then
$$\text{Var}(x_t) = \frac{\alpha_0}{1-\alpha_1}$$
In ARCH (1) model variance of next period depends on the squared residuals of last period. Therefore in order to avoid complications while studying large square residual values GARCH model is introduced.

Below is the equation of GARCH (1,1) models
$$\sigma_t^2 = \alpha_0 + \alpha_1 x_{t-1}^2 + \beta_1 \sigma_{t-1}^2$$

α_0, α_1 and β_1 should be greater than zero. Sum of α_1 and β_1 should be lesser than 1. Effect of squared residuals of last period and forecast of last period is used to calculate the next period's variance forecast.

When x_t is stationary process then
$$\text{Var}(x_t) = \frac{\alpha_0}{1-\alpha_1 - \beta_1}$$

Example 5.1: ARCH/GARCH model for ASPI data

All Share Price Index (ASPI) is one of the principle stock indices of the Colombo stock exchange in Sri Lanka. ASPI measures the movement of share prices of all listed companies. It is based on market capitalization. The main goal of this study is to fit an appropriate model that best describe ASPI volatility. ASPI monthly data from 2006 to 2015 are used for this analysis and the data during the time span from 2006 to 2014 is used to model building while the rest which is from 2014 to 2015 is used for the model validation. Corresponding data set can be found in the excel sheet .

First test data only from 2006 to 2014. Change the range from start date 2006M01 to end date 2014M12

Note : Use below steps while building a model and writing related reports.

Analyzing All Share Price Index Data

Let's first calculate the descriptive statistics of the data given. We can calculate descriptive statistics using statistics software easily.

Table 1: All Share Price Index Data

	ASPI
Mean	4404.563
Median	4722.305
Maximum	7798
Minimum	1503.02
Std. Dev.	1945.224
Skewness	0.068341
Kurtosis	1.407194
Jarque-Bera	11.50071
Probability	0.003182
Observations	108

According to the above descriptive statistics table , the range of ASPI varied from 1503 to 7798. The highest recorded in February 2011 and the lowest reported in December 2008. The data series is not normally distributed as Jarque Bera test statistic is significant (0.00<0.05) null hypothesis of data series is normally distributed get rejected. In order to examine the temporal variability of the ASPI values, the time series plot is obtained as below.

Time Series plot of ASPI values

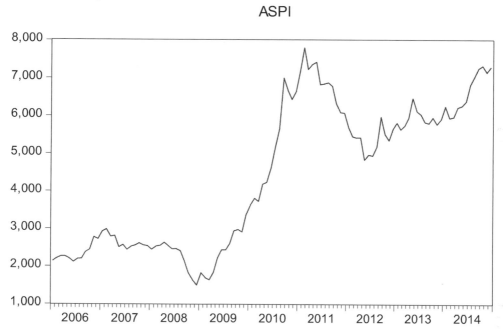

The time series plot for ASPI values are varied in low range from 2006 to 2008 and it can be seen gradual increment of the ASPI (2011), A steady decline up to May 2012. As shown in the figure 1, it can be clearly identifies a growth of ASPI after May 2012. Overall, the increasing trend pattern of ASPI can be identified over the considered time period from 2006 to 2015 and it can be claimed that the observed data series is not stationary.

Model Fitting

The data during the time span from 2006 to 2014 is used to model fitting purpose. Data from 2014 to 2015 is kept for model validation. First let's test if the data series is stationary.

Test for stationary

The ACF function is obtained using original data series from 2006 to 2014. If we look at the Autocorrelation it shows that the series is not stationary as it has a long and slow decay of lags. This shows a trend in original data series.

Autocorrelation Function for ASPI Data

Autocorrelation	Partial Correlation		AC	PAC	Q-Stat	Prob
		1	0.975	0.975	112.15	0.000
		2	0.950	-0.007	219.59	0.000
		3	0.923	-0.047	322.00	0.000
		4	0.893	-0.091	418.64	0.000
		5	0.861	-0.046	509.33	0.000
		6	0.821	-0.175	592.59	0.000
		7	0.784	0.024	669.08	0.000
		8	0.742	-0.091	738.30	0.000
		9	0.699	-0.023	800.41	0.000
		10	0.657	-0.029	855.66	0.000
		11	0.618	0.084	905.00	0.000
		12	0.581	0.014	949.02	0.000
		13	0.545	0.037	988.22	0.000
		14	0.512	0.008	1023.1	0.000
		15	0.481	0.027	1054.3	0.000
		16	0.452	-0.018	1082.1	0.000
		17	0.421	-0.071	1106.5	0.000
		18	0.393	-0.011	1127.9	0.000
		19	0.366	-0.018	1146.6	0.000
		20	0.339	-0.028	1162.9	0.000
		21	0.314	0.015	1177.0	0.000
		22	0.291	0.027	1189.3	0.000
		23	0.273	0.086	1200.2	0.000
		24	0.257	0.036	1210.0	0.000

Notice that the probability column of the above figure is zero. Non stationary data shows a probability of zero or near zero for ACF and PACF.

This outcome can further be confirmed by the dickey fuller test which is a unit root test.

Unit Root Test

		t-Statistic	Prob.*
Null Hypothesis: ASPI has a unit root			
Exogenous: Constant			
Lag Length: 0 (Automatic - based on SIC, maxlag=12)			
Augmented Dickey-Fuller test statistic		-0.467565	0.8921
Test critical values:	1% level	-3.492523	
	5% level	-2.888669	
	10% level	-2.581313	
*MacKinnon (1996) one-sided p-values.			

Hypothesis

H_0 : ASPI time series has a unit root

H_1 : ASPI time series doesn't have a unit root

The results of Dicky Fuller test further confirms that the observed series is not stationary as the test statistic is not significant at 5% of significance level (-0.467565, p-value 0.8921) under null hypothesis of ASPI data has a unit root. Therefore let's check the first difference for the stationary.

Stationary of the First Difference

Note : First create the first differenced series using statistical software or else select the first difference option.

Below table shows the first difference of the ASPI data series is stationary at 5% of significance level (-9.964197, p-value 0.0000)

		t-Statistic	Prob.*
Null Hypothesis: D(ASPI) has a unit root			
Exogenous: Constant			
Lag Length: 0 (Automatic - based on SIC, maxlag=12)			
Augmented Dickey-Fuller test statistic		-9.087859	0.0000
Test critical values:	1% level	-3.493129	
	5% level	-2.888932	
	10% level	-2.581453	
*MacKinnon (1996) one-sided p-values.			

Hypothesis

H_0 : First Differenced Series has a unit root

H_1 : First Differenced Series doesn't have a unit root

Let's check the time series of first difference and ACF function for further confirmation.

If you draw a horizontal line from 0 point of the graph , you can see that the time series is somewhat equally spread around the zero line. This is an indication of a time series being stationary.

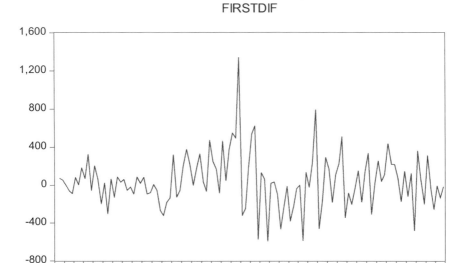

ACF and PACF of the first difference of ASPI Data.

Autocorrelation	Partial Correlation		AC	PAC	Q-Stat	Prob
		1	0.075	0.075	0.6531	0.419
		2	0.013	0.008	0.6741	0.714
		3	0.175	0.175	4.3402	0.227
		4	0.140	0.119	6.7031	0.152
		5	0.201	0.193	11.603	0.041
		6	-0.074	-0.131	12.277	0.056
		7	0.134	0.117	14.489	0.043
		8	0.111	0.010	16.015	0.042
		9	-0.043	-0.061	16.251	0.062
		10	-0.098	-0.164	17.481	0.064
		11	-0.081	-0.087	18.317	0.075
		12	0.020	-0.039	18.368	0.105

Notice that the probability column of the above figure is not zero. Stationary data is not significant.

Autocorrelation Function for the first difference of ASPI Data shows that the first four correlations are not significant, but the fifth autocorrelation is significant (0.041). Random walk therefore a series is stationary. As you can see in time series plot of first difference, there still is some pattern.

We can try taking the second difference to see if there is any improvement.

Taking the Second Difference

In order to make the time series more stationary we take the second difference of the above data set and plot it as in the below figure. If you draw zero line in the plot, the variance is almost equally spread besides the zero line.

Time Series Plot of Second Difference

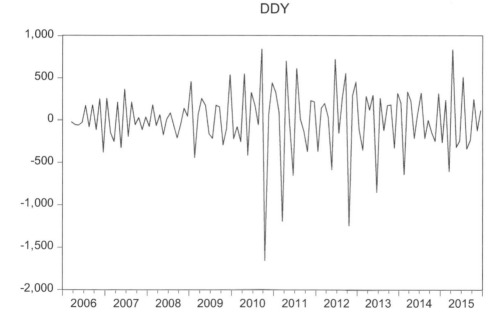

ACF and PACF Plot of Second Difference

Autocorrelation	Partial Correlation		AC	PAC	Q-Stat	Prob
		1	-0.437	-0.437	20.786	0.000
		2	-0.160	-0.433	23.598	0.000
		3	0.109	-0.274	24.914	0.000
		4	-0.050	-0.304	25.190	0.000
		5	0.189	0.039	29.259	0.000
		6	-0.260	-0.216	37.007	0.000
		7	0.104	-0.087	38.260	0.000
		8	0.110	0.015	39.669	0.000
		9	-0.071	0.103	40.267	0.000
		10	-0.053	-0.004	40.596	0.000
		11	-0.032	-0.034	40.720	0.000
		12	0.059	-0.124	41.146	0.000
		13	0.065	-0.006	41.663	0.000
		14	-0.088	-0.035	42.626	0.000
		15	-0.071	-0.156	43.256	0.000
		16	0.158	-0.032	46.423	0.000
		17	0.015	0.101	46.453	0.000
		18	-0.252	-0.223	54.717	0.000
		19	0.220	0.045	61.091	0.000
		20	0.013	0.068	61.112	0.000
		21	-0.037	0.083	61.294	0.000
		22	-0.081	-0.045	62.194	0.000
		23	-0.102	-0.201	63.615	0.000
		24	0.290	-0.097	75.332	0.000

Partial autocorrelation function (PACF) implies AR (2) signature as the first two spikes are prominent. We can test AR(1) and AR(2) models for this data series. Then in ACF function 1st lag and 6th lag are significant.

Dickey-Fuller Test for Second Difference of the time series

Null Hypothesis: D(ASPI,2) has a unit root			
Exogenous: Constant			
Lag Length: 3 (Automatic - based on SIC, maxlag=12)			
		t-Statistic	Prob.*
Augmented Dickey-Fuller test statistic		-10.06325	0.0000
Test critical values:	1% level	-3.491345	
	5% level	-2.888157	
	10% level	-2.581041	
*MacKinnon (1996) one-sided p-values.			

Hypothesis

H_0 :Second difference has a unit root

H_1 :Second difference doesn't have a unit root

Figure 3.2 shows that Ho is rejected. Therefore we can conclude that the first difference of the data series is stationary.

Now we can try to fit a model for the above series.

Fit AR (1) Model

AR Model for second differenced data

Dependent Variable: D(ASPI,2)				
Method: Least Squares				
Sample (adjusted): 2006M04 2014M12				
Included observations: 105 after adjustments				
Convergence achieved after 3 iterations				

Variable	Coefficient	Std. Error	t-Statistic	Prob.
C	-0.099070	23.42731	-0.004229	0.9966
AR(1)	-0.439562	0.088870	-4.946154	0.0000

R-squared	0.191931	Mean dependent var	0.889810
Adjusted R-squared	0.184086	S.D. dependent var	382.5761
S.E. of regression	345.5731	Akaike info criterion	14.54715
Sum squared resid	12300340	Schwarz criterion	14.59770
Log likelihood	-761.7253	Hannan-Quinn criter.	14.56763
F-statistic	24.46444	Durbin-Watson stat	2.376571
Prob(F-statistic)	0.000003		

| Inverted AR Roots | -.44 | | |

H_0 : AR(1) Model is not significant
H_1 :AR(1) Model is significant

Above Figure shows that the parameter of AR(1) model is significant as the probability is lesser than the significant level of 5%. As the parameter is significant now we have to check for the residual test of the above fitted model to identify if the model is suitable for further forecasting.

Residual Check for AR Model
Randomness of the Residuals

Correlogram of the AR Model

Autocorrelation	Partial Correlation		AC	PAC	Q-Stat	Prob
		1	0.255	0.255	7.0048	0.008
		2	0.107	0.045	8.2529	0.016
		3	0.144	0.114	10.543	0.014
		4	0.101	0.039	11.685	0.020
		5	0.318	0.295	23.075	0.000
		6	0.108	-0.056	24.411	0.000
		7	0.006	-0.048	24.415	0.001
		8	0.107	0.058	25.750	0.001
		9	0.030	-0.036	25.854	0.002
		10	-0.029	-0.139	25.952	0.004
		11	-0.029	-0.028	26.052	0.006
		12	0.004	0.053	26.055	0.011

Every probability value of residual is not greater than 0.05 (not significant) , therefore null hypothesis of , residuals are random fails. The AR model cannot be accepted.

Test statistics of the Durbin Watson Test is also 2.3765 as mentioned in the table of outputs related to AR Model for second differenced data. Therefore we can conclude that data is not random.

Heteroscedasticity Tests
Breush Godfrey LM test is done to identify the heteroscedasticity of the model. Apply this test using statistical software to the AR model.

Breusch-Godfrey Serial Correlation LM Test:			
F-statistic	4.540191	Prob. F(12,91)	0.0000
Obs*R-squared	39.32190	Prob. Chi-Square(12)	0.0001

Below hypothesis are tested by the Breusch-Godfrey Heteroscedasticity test.

H_0 : There is no serial correlation

H_1 : There is serial correlation

Above table shows that the alternate hypothesis is accepted (Probability is significant). As it is concluded to have an ARCH effect we can try to fit ARCH/GARCH Model.

We can also use Heteroskedasticity Test for ARCH effects as well to identify any heteroskedasticity as shown in below.

Heteroskedasticity Test: ARCH

F-statistic	7.093548	Prob. F(1,102)	0.0090
Obs*R-squared	6.762352	Prob. Chi-Square(1)	0.0093

Test Equation:
Dependent Variable: RESID^2
Method: Least Squares
Sample (adjusted): 2006M05 2014M12
Included observations: 104 after adjustments

Variable	Coefficient	Std. Error	t-Statistic	Prob.
C	88201.60	26234.60	3.362034	0.0011
RESID^2(-1)	0.254845	0.095685	2.663372	0.0090

R-squared	0.065023	Mean dependent var	118235.4
Adjusted R-squared	0.055856	S.D. dependent var	248607.8
S.E. of regression	241564.9	Akaike info criterion	27.64671
Sum squared resid	5.95E+12	Schwarz criterion	27.69756
Log likelihood	-1435.629	Hannan-Quinn criter.	27.66731
F-statistic	7.093548	Durbin-Watson stat	2.024234
Prob(F-statistic)	0.008992		

Note that there is a serial correlation of residuals of second difference. Heteroskedasticity test is also significant. It is better to fit a ARCH model for the dataset.

Next step is to identify a model for variation of the data set as there is a serial correlation.

Check AR (2) model for the data set.

If you use eviews use "d(aspi,2) c ar(2)" for model estimation code.

According to ACF and PACF Plot of Second Difference, there is an indication of possibility of AR(2) signature. Therefore we can test a model for AR(2) signature as shown in below table. But the table shows that model is not significant.

Dependent Variable: D(ASPI,2)
Method: Least Squares
Sample (adjusted): 2006M05 2014M12
Included observations: 104 after adjustments
Convergence achieved after 3 iterations

Variable	Coefficient	Std. Error	t-Statistic	Prob.
C	1.210077	32.18551	0.037597	0.9701
AR(2)	-0.161547	0.098242	-1.644372	0.1032

R-squared	0.025825	Mean dependent var	1.404038
Adjusted R-squared	0.016274	S.D. dependent var	384.3923
S.E. of regression	381.2516	Akaike info criterion	14.74384
Sum squared resid	14825986	Schwarz criterion	14.79469
Log likelihood	-764.6797	Hannan-Quinn criter.	14.76444
F-statistic	2.703960	Durbin-Watson stat	3.021406
Prob(F-statistic)	0.103178		

Inverted AR Roots	-.00+.40i	-.00-.40i

ARCH(1) MODEL

According to above tables, there is a serial correlation in the series. Therefore ARCH(1) model is tested for the data series. The standard variance model for the ARCH (1) series is $\sigma^2 = \alpha_0 + \alpha_1 u_{t-1}^2$

Eviews Command : Equation Estimation d(aspi,2) c ar(1)
Select ARCH 1 effect and GARCH 0 effect.

113

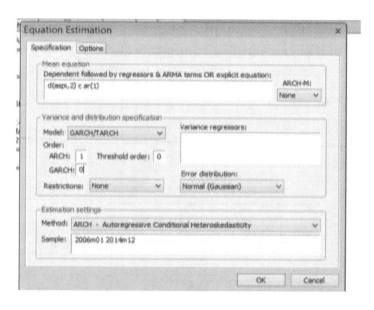

OUTPUT : ARCH (1,1) model

Dependent Variable: D(ASPI,2)
Method: ML - ARCH (Marquardt) - Normal distribution
Sample (adjusted): 2006M04 2014M12
Included observations: 105 after adjustments
Convergence achieved after 49 iterations
Presample variance: backcast (parameter = 0.7)
GARCH = C(3) + C(4)*RESID(-1)^2

Variable	Coefficient	Std. Error	z-Statistic	Prob.
C	-6.420257	20.09460	-0.319502	0.7493
AR(1)	-0.502247	0.124307	-4.040382	0.0001
Variance Equation				
C	70715.13	12246.15	5.774480	0.0000
RESID(-1)^2	0.436720	0.232354	1.879541	0.0602

R-squared	0.187425	Mean dependent var	0.889810
Adjusted R-squared	0.179536	S.D. dependent var	382.5761
S.E. of regression	346.5355	Akaike info criterion	14.46110
Sum squared resid	12368943	Schwarz criterion	14.56220
Log likelihood	-755.2077	Hannan-Quinn criter.	14.50207
Durbin-Watson stat	2.307585		

Inverted AR Roots	-.50

114

Variance equation $\sigma^2 = 72184.73 + 0.4226u_{t-1}^2$ from figure 5.1 cannot be accepted as the parameter of the ARCH effect of the model is not significant at 95% significance level as it's p-value is 0.0602.

But according to Figure 4.2.2 the data set shows a serial correlation. Therefore we can try fitting a GARCH Model.

GARCH(1,1) Model

Below figure shows the outcome of fitting a GARCH(1,1) Model.

Dependent Variable: D(ASPI,2)
Method: ML - ARCH (Marquardt) - Normal distribution
Sample (adjusted): 2006M04 2014M12
Included observations: 105 after adjustments
Convergence achieved after 32 iterations
Presample variance: backcast (parameter = 0.7)
GARCH = C(3) + C(4)*RESID(-1)^2 + C(5)*GARCH(-1)

Variable	Coefficient	Std. Error	z-Statistic	Prob.
C	-5.454464	14.07396	-0.387557	0.6983
AR(1)	-0.566640	0.115028	-4.926112	0.0000
Variance Equation				
C	2945.298	2417.814	1.218166	0.2232
RESID(-1)^2	0.259429	0.129792	1.998802	0.0456
GARCH(-1)	0.750510	0.099179	7.567222	0.0000

R-squared	0.175437	Mean dependent var	0.889810
Adjusted R-squared	0.167432	S.D. dependent var	382.5761
S.E. of regression	349.0823	Akaike info criterion	14.25049
Sum squared resid	12551417	Schwarz criterion	14.37687
Log likelihood	-743.1506	Hannan-Quinn criter.	14.30170
Durbin-Watson stat	2.245785		
Inverted AR Roots	-.57		

Variance Equation shows that the parameters of the GARCH model is significant with p-value of 0.0000 (GARCH effect)and p-value of 0.0456 (ARCH effect). Mean Equation shows that the AR(1) Model is also significant.

Residual check on GARCH (1,1) model should be done to check if the model can be used for future predictions and analyzing the data.

$$\sigma^2 = \alpha_0 + \alpha_1 u_{t-1}^2 + \beta_1 \sigma_{t-1}^2$$
$$\sigma^2 = 2945.298 + 0.2594 u_{t-1}^2 + 0.7505 \sigma_{t-1}^2$$

RESIDUAL CHECK FOR GARCH(1,1)
Correlogram Squared Residuals

Autocorrelation	Partial Correlation		AC	PAC	Q-Stat	Prob
		1	0.112	0.112	1.4395	
		2	-0.051	-0.064	1.7387	0.187
		3	-0.004	0.010	1.7404	0.419
		4	0.074	0.071	2.3884	0.496
		5	-0.024	-0.042	2.4565	0.652
		6	0.011	0.027	2.4700	0.781
		7	-0.098	-0.108	3.6386	0.725
		8	-0.017	0.004	3.6760	0.816
		9	-0.001	-0.006	3.6760	0.885
		10	-0.088	-0.096	4.6442	0.864
		11	0.013	0.056	4.6672	0.912
		12	-0.120	-0.153	6.4914	0.839
		13	-0.115	-0.077	8.2095	0.769
		14	-0.020	-0.007	8.2594	0.826
		15	-0.014	-0.046	8.2851	0.874
		16	-0.089	-0.059	9.3328	0.859
		17	-0.077	-0.090	10.130	0.860
		18	0.052	0.072	10.504	0.881
		19	-0.036	-0.090	10.680	0.907
		20	0.216	0.236	17.156	0.579
		21	0.089	0.038	18.269	0.570
		22	0.113	0.098	20.069	0.517
		23	-0.041	-0.060	20.307	0.564
		24	0.142	0.121	23.229	0.447
		25	0.083	0.057	24.249	0.447
		26	0.079	0.028	25.182	0.452
		27	-0.133	-0.102	27.839	0.366
		28	-0.138	-0.148	30.730	0.282

Figure: ACF or PACF of RESIDUALS OF GARCH (1,1).

H_0 :Squared Residuals are random

H_1 :Squared Residuals are not random

At some lags of Figure 5.1.1 it shows that the p values of residuals are greater than 0.05.Therefore the residuals are random.

Heteroskedasticity Test

Heteroskedasticity Test: ARCH				
F-statistic	0.582269	Prob. F(3,105)		0.6279
Obs*R-squared	1.783678	Prob. Chi-Square(3)		0.6185

Test Equation
Dependent Variable: WGT_RESID^2
Method: Least Squares
Sample (adjusted): 2006M07 2015M07
Included observations: 109 after adjustments

Variable	Coefficient	Std. Error	t-Statistic	Prob.
C	0.950920	0.213344	4.457218	0.0000
WGT_RESID^2(-1)	0.117029	0.097459	1.200805	0.2325
WGT_RESID^2(-2)	-0.067396	0.097989	-0.687795	0.4931
WGT_RESID^2(-3)	0.009814	0.097510	0.100643	0.9200

R-squared	0.016364	Mean dependent var	1.011130
Adjusted R-squared	-0.011740	S.D. dependent var	1.481669
S.E. of regression	1.490341	Akaike info criterion	3.671894
Sum squared resid	233.2173	Schwarz criterion	3.770659
Log likelihood	-196.1182	Hannan-Quinn criter.	3.711947
F-statistic	0.582269	Durbin-Watson stat	1.992815
Prob(F-statistic)	0.627936		

H_0 : There is no arch effect

H_1: There is arch effect

Chi-Square probability as shown in Heteroskedasticity test is 0.5390 is greater than 0.05, therefore we can conclude that there is no ARCH effect in the model which is a good sign.

Normality of the Residuals

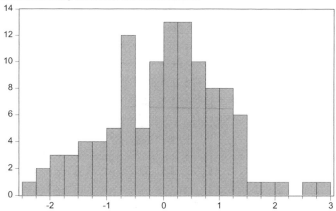

Series: Standardized Residuals
Sample 2006M04 2015M07
Observations 112

Mean	0.054770
Median	0.153396
Maximum	2.968109
Minimum	-2.406043
Std. Dev.	0.999404
Skewness	-0.014203
Kurtosis	3.164184
Jarque-Bera	0.129562
Probability	0.937273

H_0 : Residuals are normally distributed

H_1 : Residuals are not normally distributed.

Previous figure shows that the probability of Jarque-Bera test (0.665489) is greater than 0.05, therefore H_0 is not rejected.

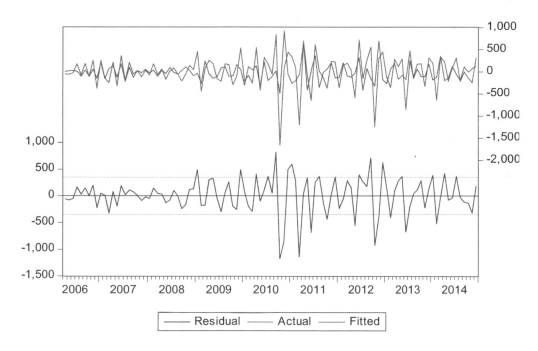

118

6. Conclusion

Time Series Model with GARCH(1,1) effect can be used for the data set. Therefore
Estimation Equation:

$$\sigma^2 = \alpha_0 + \alpha_1 u_{t-1}^2 + \beta_1 \sigma_{t-1}^2$$
$$\sigma^2 = 2945.298 + 0.2594 u_{t-1}^2 + 0.7505 \sigma_{t-1}^2$$

7. VALIDATE THE MODEL

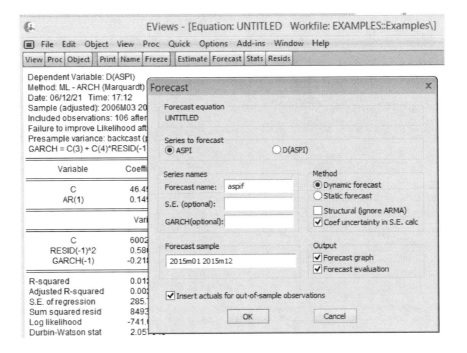

Percentage error table

Time	ASPI	Estimated ASPI	Percentage Error = (Estimated ASPI-ASPI)/ASPI*100%
Jan-15	7180.10	7255.36	1.05
Feb-15	7301.30	7310.13	0.12
Mar-15	6820.30	7300.59	7.04
Apr-15	7179.00	7318.94	1.95
May-15	7220.30	7312.94	1.28
Jun-15	7020.80	7312.20	4.15
Jul-15	7332.10	7299.93	-0.44
Aug-15	7306.90	7285.65	-0.29
Sep-15	7050.90	7263.96	3.02
Oct-15	7042.10	7237.93	2.78
Nov-15	6909.20	7205.81	4.29
Dec-15	6894.50	7168.60	3.98

Percentage Error is almost between ± 10 %. Therefore we can assume that the model is fit to do forecasting.

Below figure shows that the forecasted series falls between two standard deviation therefore, the forecasted series has confidence level of 95%.

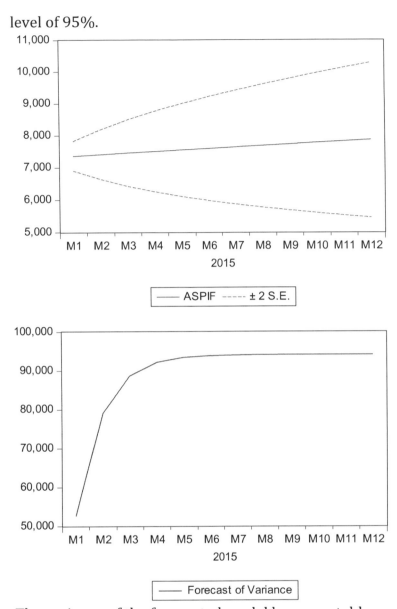

The variance of the forecasted model become stable

Chapter Six
Vector Auto-Regression Model and Vector Error Correction Model

6.1 Vector Auto Regression Model

Vector Auto-Regression Model and Vector Error correction models are used for multivariate time series data analysis. It captures the linear interdependencies among multiple time series. VAR models checks the influences of their own lags and lags of the other variables of time series. In VAR models there is no specific endogenous and exogenous variable.

Given below is a simple bivariate first order VAR model.

$$Y_{1,t} = \beta_{10} + \beta_{11} Y_{1,t\text{-}1} + \alpha_{11} Y_{2,t\text{-}1} + u_{1,t}$$
$$Y_{2,t} = \beta_{20} + \beta_{21} Y_{2,t\text{-}1} + \alpha_{21} Y_{1,t\text{-}1} + u_{2,t}$$

$u_{1,t}$ and $u_{2,t}$ are white noise disturbances with standard deviation σ_{y1} and σ_{y2} respectively.

Above equation in matrix form

$$\begin{pmatrix} Y_{1,t} \\ Y_{2,t} \end{pmatrix} = \begin{pmatrix} \beta_{10} \\ \beta_{20} \end{pmatrix} + \begin{pmatrix} \beta_{11} & \alpha_{11} \\ \alpha_{21} & \beta_{21} \end{pmatrix} \begin{pmatrix} Y_{1,t-1} \\ Y_{2,t-1} \end{pmatrix} + \begin{pmatrix} u_{1,t} \\ u_{2,t} \end{pmatrix}$$

In simple form it is

$$Y_t = \beta_0 + \beta_1 Y_{t\text{-}1} + u_t$$

β_0 – Vector Error Constant

β_1 – Matrix of autoregressive coefficient

u_t – Vector generalization of white noise

Assumptions

All the variables in VAR model are stationary (this avoids understandable effects, stationary assumption does not always apply to white noise disturbance terms)

Error term of the VAR model should satisfy

*Error terms are random
*There is no serial correlation between error terms.
*Variance Covariance Matrix of the error term is zero

Economic indicators show long term relationship among variables. These time series don't have constant mean or variance because they differ according to the time. Analyzing non stationary time series will lead to erroneous results. De-trending and differentiating are two methods which are used to turn non stationary series into stationary time series.

Cintegration is a technique used to find a possible correlation between two time series in the long term. Two typical methods to which are recommended to examine long run relationship of variables are Engle and Granger (1987) co-integration test and Johansen-Juselius (1990) cointegration test. Engle and Grange test is suitable for bivariate analysis and Johansen –Juselius is suitable for multivariate analysis.

Johansen –Juselius (1990) Co-integration Test

Johansen Juselius co-integration test is used to identify the long run relationships that may exist among representative variable. It is based on VAR model of order p. In Johansen Juselius co-integration all variables are treated as endogenous variables and it doesn't segregate dependent variables and independent variables. Johansen Juselius approach is a one step approach compared to two stepped Engle Granger methodology. Due to these reasons Johansen Juselius co-integration is considered as an effective statistical method for testing co-integration.

6.2   Error Correction Model

Error Correction mechanism (ECM) is useful in modeling non-stationary data. ECM helps to separate the long run and short run dynamics; we can use error correction term when there is co-integration. Error correction term should be negative if the ECM is appropriate.

Error Correction Model is used for data with underlying variables having a long run stochastic trend or a co-integration. It estimates both long term and short term effects of one time series on another time series. Error is short run dynamics and the error correction term is long-run equilibrium.

Error correction process has an adjustment speed towards the long-run equilibrium. But in short-term there can be deviation from the equilibrium which means there can be terms that doesn't tally.

Below is the VECM equation for VAR representation.

$$\begin{pmatrix} \Delta Y_{1,t} \\ \Delta Y_{2,t} \end{pmatrix} = \begin{pmatrix} \beta_{10} \\ \beta_{20} \end{pmatrix} + \begin{pmatrix} \beta_{11} & \alpha_{11} \\ \alpha_{21} & \beta_{21} \end{pmatrix} \begin{pmatrix} Y_{1,t-1} \\ Y_{2,t-1} \end{pmatrix} + \begin{pmatrix} \beta_1 \\ \beta_2 \end{pmatrix} +$$

$$[Y_{1,t-1}, \gamma Y_{2,t-1}] + \begin{pmatrix} u_{1,t} \\ u_{2,t} \end{pmatrix}$$

$\begin{pmatrix} \beta_1 \\ \beta_2 \end{pmatrix} + [Y_{1,t-1}, \gamma Y_{2,t-1}]$ is the ECM term

Long term relationship between $Y_{1,t-1}$ and $Y_{2,t-1}$ are defined by γ.
β_1 and β_2 are error correction coefficient. β_1 and β_2 measures the speed of adjustment to equilibrium.

VAR model should be integrated in the first difference I(1). They shouldn't be integrated at level I(0), Integrated at level means stationary at level.

6.3   Granger causality

Causality is a kind of cause and effect relationship. Granger causality finds the precedence of another variable. If X and Y are two economics variables, Granger causality can test if X variable precedence (occurs before) Y variable or vice versa. Granger causality can measure the causality using probability. Assumption of the Granger causality test is that variables are independent.

Null hypothesis for Granger Causality
H_0 : x(t) doesn't Granger-cause y(t)
H_1 : x(t) does Granger-cause y(t)

Null hypothesis means lagged x-values do not explain the variation in y. ganger causality test can be done for a selected number of lags. Lags are selected according to model order selection method. Before applying this test we should make sure if the time series are stationary and do not have any unit root.

Below is the test statistic of Granger causality

$$F = \frac{(ESS_R - ESS_{UR})/q}{ESS_{UR}/(n - k)}$$

If there is a large number of variables and lag orders, then using chi-test with likelihood ratio or Wald test is better than using F test.

The long-run relationship between variables , indicate that there is Granger causality at least for one direction. There are unidirectional and bidirectional Granger Causality.

Example 6.1 : VAR Model

We are going to build a Vector Auto-regression model to model the relationship between monthly inflation rate and unemployment rate in Hong Kong from 1995 t0 2016. Find the data sheet in the Time Series Data excel sheet at the website. First let's analyze each variable separately. . The nature and descriptive statistics of the variables are identified prior advance analysis. Fin data at VARHK in excel sheet.

<u>Unemployment Rate in Hong Kong</u>

Unemployment rate in Hong Kong shows cyclic pattern. Highest unemployment rate of 8.5% is recorded in June 2000 and the lowest unemployment rate (2.1%) is reported in Sept 1997.

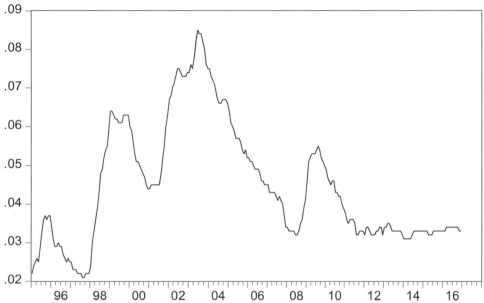

Figure 6. 1 Unemployment rate in Hong Kong from January 1995 to December 2016.

Figure 6.2 (Next Page) shows that the of Unemployment rate in Hong Kong from January 1995 to December 2016 varies from 2.1% to 8.5%. . Unemployment rate takes a mean value of 4.4% during the period and the variable is not normally distributed according to the Jarque-Bera statistics (P-Value 0.00< 0.05)

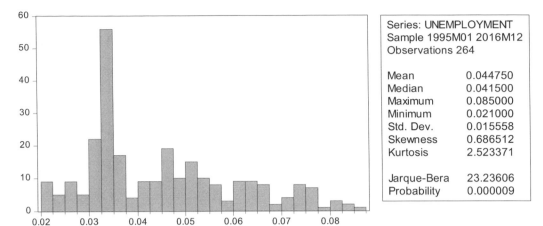

Figure 6.2 Descriptive Statistics of Unemployment rate in Hong Kong From January 1995 to December 2016

Inflation Rate of the Hong Kong

Inflation is an overall increase in Consumer Price Index. It is also the weighted average of prices for difference goods.

Figure 6.3. Inflation rate in Hong Kong from January 1995 to December 2016.

Figure 6.3 shows that from January 1995 to December 1995 inflation rate takes a higher rate over 9%. After April 2015 it takes a value below 3% except of the sudden increase of 4.26% in August 2016. It is noted that the highest unemployment rate of the period is 10.3% recorded in January 1995. Inflation rate takes the lowest of -6.1% in August 1999.

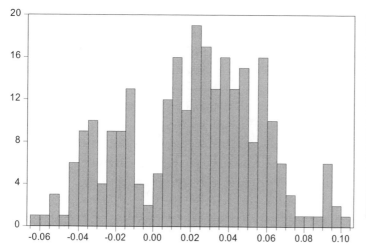

Figure 6.4 Descriptive Statistics of Inflation rate in Hong Kong From January 1995 to December 2016

Figure 6.4 shows that the of inflation rate in Hong Kong from January 1995 to December 2016 varies from (6.1%) to 10.3%. Inflation rate takes a mean value of 2.02% during the period and the variable is normally distributed according to the Jarque-Bera statistics (P-Value 0.101> 0.05).

Unemployment and Inflation in Hong Kong
It is important for the Hong Kong policy makers to know about the relationship between unemployment and inflation

According to the Figure 6.5 (next page) a distinct gap between inflation and unemployment of Hong Kong is clearly seen December

1995 to November 2007. On February 2009 the unemployment rate and inflation rate takes an equal value of 0.036.

Figure 6.5 Unemployment rate and Inflation rate in Hong Kong from January 1995 to December 2016.

Table 6.1 Months showing narrow gap between Inflation Rate and Unemployment rate in Hong Kong from January 1995 to December 2016

Year and Month	Inflation Rate	Unemployment Rate
1998 June	0.04	0.043
2007 November	0.034	0.037
2008 September	0.03	0.035
2012 June	0.037	0.032
2012 August	0.037	0.033
2013 January	0.03	0.034
2015 June	0.0356	0.032

Table 6.1 can be created using the figure 6.5 or the data set. These kinds of tables are valuable in data analysis prior modeling, in order to describe the data set.

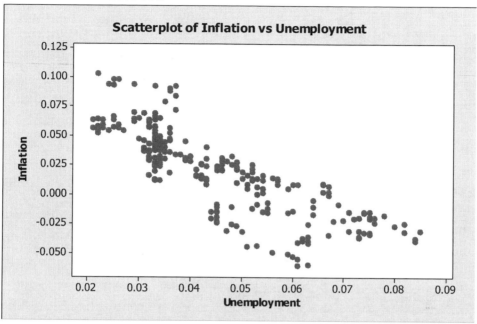

Figure 6.6: Scatter Plot of Unemployment rate vs Inflation rate in Hong Kong from January 1995 to December 2016

Figure 6.6 plots monthly unemployment rate and inflation rate in Hong Kong together for January 1995 to December 2016. These data suggest that there isa trade-off relationship between Unemployment and Inflation in Hong Kong as William Phillips explained in Phillips Curve theorem. It is important to confirm the inverse relationship between Inflation rate and Unemployment rate using a statistical model.

Inflation rate and unemployment rates are two economic times series variables. It is important to check interdependencies among these time series variables. We cannot identify a dependent, independent variable separately in this case. Therefore it is suggested that we can use a VAR model.

Unit Root Test

Eviews Command : Select both variables > Open as Group > View >
Unit root test > Individual root-FISHER –PP > Then we can test unit
root for both level and 1ˢᵗ difference separately.

In table 6.2 , it is shown the Augmented Dicky-Fuller test results of
each level under the Null Hypothesis of Variable has a unit root. If
Variable has a unit root then the data is not stationary. According to
the test results shown in the table 6.2 it can be identified that at 5% of
significance level both variables are not stationary at level and both
variables are stationary at First Difference.

Table 6.2: Augmented Dicky Fuller test results

variable	Level	first difference
Inflation	0.2695	0.0000
unemployment	0.2752	0.0000

Eviews Command : Open data set using VAR.

VAR Model Selection

In E-views, before application of any VAR model, it is needed to open
data with VAR model as default. But we are going to ignore the output
we get in this stage.

Lag Length Criteria

Before running a VAR model it is important to identify the suitable lag
order for the model. Since monthly unemployment rate and inflation
rate are taken for the study, 12 lags are checked.

Purpose of lag augmentation is to eliminate the autocorrelation,
sometimes low lag orders suffer from serial correlation.

Best fitting lag structure should be identified to fit a most suitable
model. Most common methods to identify the model is using Akaike
Information Criteria (AIC) ,Schwartz Baysian (SC) and Hannan-Quinn
(HQ).Two criterion identify two as most suitable VAR lag order.

Therefore Lag Order of 2 is used for further model building.(* indicates lag order selected by the criterion) AIC identifies 5 as the best lag order, SC and HQ identifies 2. Likelihood ratio identifies 12. (Next page , table 6.2)

Eviews Command : View > Lag structure > Lag length Criteria > 12 lags

Table 6.2 VAR Lag Order Selection Criteria

VAR Lag Order Selection Criteria
Endogenous variables: INFLATION UNEMPLOYMENT
Exogenous variables: C
Sample: 1995M01 2016M12
Included observations: 252

Lag	LogL	LR	FPE	AIC	SC	HQ
0	1346.229	NA	7.98e-08	-10.66848	-10.64047	-10.65721
1	2122.961	1534.971	1.73e-10	-16.80128	-16.71724	-16.76746
2	2187.663	126.8365	1.07e-10	-17.28304	-17.14298*	-17.22668*
3	2191.740	7.927450	1.07e-10	-17.28365	-17.08757	-17.20475
4	2194.802	5.904624	1.08e-10	-17.27620	-17.02410	-17.17476
5	2200.696	11.27489	1.06e-10*	-17.29124*	-16.98312	-17.16726
6	2202.409	3.248894	1.08e-10	-17.27309	-16.90894	-17.12656
7	2203.636	2.306883	1.10e-10	-17.25108	-16.83091	-17.08201
8	2207.587	7.370108	1.10e-10	-17.25069	-16.77450	-17.05908
9	2211.073	6.446219	1.11e-10	-17.24661	-16.71440	-17.03246
10	2214.986	7.173107	1.11e-10	-17.24592	-16.65768	-17.00922
11	2215.349	0.659238	1.14e-10	-17.21705	-16.57279	-16.95781
12	2224.019	15.61974*	1.10e-10	-17.25412	-16.55383	-16.97234

* indicates lag order selected by the criterion
LR: sequential modified LR test statistic (each test at 5% level)
FPE: Final prediction error
AIC: Akaike information criterion
SC: Schwarz information criterion
HQ: Hannan-Quinn information criterion

VAR MODEL SELECTION

COINTEGRATION TEST
VAR Residual Serial Correlation LM Test is done (Table 6.4, next page) to confirm the selected lag order is according to the null hypothesis of no serial correlation at lag order h. Second order auto correlation is not significant at 5% significance level (P- value ,0.7897>0.05). Therefore it further confirms second order lag structure can be used as a fitting model.

Table 6.4 VAR Residual Serial Correlation LM Tests

VAR Residual Serial Correlation LM Tests
Null Hypothesis: no serial correlation at lag order h
Sample: 1995M01 2016M12
Included observations: 262

Lags	LM-Stat	Prob
1	6.594240	0.1589
2	1.705535	0.7897
3	2.499028	0.6448
4	7.724531	0.1022
5	9.380223	0.0523
6	1.424507	0.8399
7	8.522728	0.0742
8	4.360527	0.3594
9	5.541875	0.2361
10	1.111148	0.8925
11	7.552979	0.1094
12	71.07117	0.0000

Probs from chi-square with 4 df.

Co-Integration Test

VAR model is used to forecast and describe multivariate time series data which are stationary. Existence of Co-integration indicates that data are non stationary. If the data are non-stationary Vector Error Correction model should be used. Existence of Co-Integration is tested using Johansen Co-Integration test.

Before applying co-integration test it is needed to identify the stationary of the given series separately. If level Series is non-stationary and first difference is stationary Co-integration test can be applied to times series data.

Co-integration is applied to identify if the both variables are stationary and which model from VAR and VECM should be applied for the variables. Test is done under the null hypothesis of "there is r co-integration between inflation and unemployment"

Table 6.6: Johansen Co-Integration Test Summary of all five assumptions

Sample: 1995M01 2016M12
Included observations: 261
Series: INFLATION UNEMPLOYMENT
Lags interval: 1 to 2

Selected (0.05 level*) Number of Cointegrating Relations by Model

Data Trend:	None	None	Linear	Linear	Quadratic
Test Type	No Intercept	Intercept	Intercept	Intercept	Intercept
	No Trend	No Trend	No Trend	Trend	Trend
Trace	0	0	0	0	0
Max-Eig	0	0	0	0	0

*Critical values based on MacKinnon-Haug-Michelis (1999)
Information Criteria by Rank and Model

Data Trend:	None	None	Linear	Linear	Quadratic
Rank or	No Intercept	Intercept	Intercept	Intercept	Intercept
No. of CEs	No Trend	No Trend	No Trend	Trend	Trend
	Log Likelihood by Rank (rows) and Model (columns)				
0	2259.108	2259.108	2259.380	2259.380	2259.873
1	2262.242	2263.778	2263.806	2263.807	2264.270
2	2262.537	2266.102	2266.102	2267.219	2267.219
	Akaike Information Criteria by Rank (rows) and Model (columns)				
0	-17.24987*	17.24987*	-17.23663	-17.23663	-17.22508
1	-17.24324	-17.24734	-17.23989	-17.23224	-17.22812
2	-17.21484	-17.22684	-17.22684	-17.22007	-17.22007

	Schwarz Criteria by Rank (rows) and Model (columns)				
0	-17.14061*	-17.14061*	-17.10006	-17.10006	-17.06120
1	-17.07935	-17.06980	-17.04869	-17.02738	-17.00961
2	-16.99633	-16.98101	-16.98101	-16.94693	-16.94693

According to the table 6.6, all five types of Co-Integration test are applied for the most suitable lag structure of 2. It can be identified that there is no co-integration in variables. Data series are already stationary. Therefore a VAR (P) model should be applied to identify the relationship between the variables.P or the lag order is two as already selected.

VAR(2) Model

Lag order of two is used to calculate the VAR model.

Table 6.7: VAR(2) Model estimates

Vector Autoregression Estimates
Sample (adjusted): 1995M03 2016M12
Included observations: 262 after adjustments
Standard errors in ( ) & t-statistics in [ ]

	INFLATION	UNEMPLOYMENT
INFLATION(-1)	0.726082	-0.017193
	(0.06097)	(0.01020)
	[11.9087]	[-1.68586]
INFLATION(-2)	0.206498	0.014063
	(0.06041)	(0.01010)
	[3.41846]	[1.39180]
UNEMPLOYMENT(-1)	-1.067401	1.571636
	(0.30055)	(0.05027)
	[-3.55145]	[31.2626]
UNEMPLOYMENT(-2)	0.963779	-0.586717
	(0.30282)	(0.05065)
	[3.18270]	[-11.5836]
C	0.005655	0.000744
	(0.00298)	(0.00050)
	[1.90031]	[1.49536]

R-squared	0.950914	0.992950
Adj. R-squared	0.950150	0.992840
Sum sq. resids	0.015802	0.000442
S.E. equation	0.007841	0.001312
F-statistic	1244.677	9048.868
Log likelihood	901.0307	1369.533
Akaike AIC	-6.839929	-10.41628
Schwarz SC	-6.771831	-10.34819
Mean dependent	0.019701	0.044916
S.D. dependent	0.035120	0.015500
Determinant resid covariance (dof adj.)		1.05E-10
Determinant resid covariance		1.01E-10
Log likelihood		2271.765
Akaike information criterion		-17.26538
Schwarz criterion		-17.12919

In table 6.7 VAR model is estimated using lag order 2. T statistics shown in the squared brackets should be greater than 2 for lag order to be significant or the lag order to be have an effect on the variable. According to the table 6.7 one period and two periods lagged unemployment rate has effect on Unemployment rate and Inflation Rate. Further it can be identified that one period and two periods lagged inflation have effect on inflation rate but not on Unemployment rate.

Below 2 equations can be derived from the model shown in table 5.4.1

MODEL 1

inflation = 0.7261*inflation(-1) + 0.2065*inflation(-2) - 1.0674*unemployment(-1) + 0.9638*unemployment(-2) + 0.0057

MODEL 2

unemployment = - 0.0172*inflation(-1) + 0.0141*inflation(-2) + 1.5716*unemployment(-1) - 0.5867*unemployment(-2) + 0.0007

The models which are derived using VAR methods should be tested for its accuracy and validity.

Testing Model 1

Model 1 identifies the inflation as the forecasting variable and inflation is calculated using first, second lagged series of unemployment and inflation.

inflation = 0.7261*inflation(-1) + 0.2065*inflation(-2) - 1.0674*unemployment(-1) + 0.9638*unemployment(-2) + 0.0057

Significance of The Model

Table 6.8 Testing the significance of the Model

Dependent Variable: INFLATION
Method: Least Squares
Sample (adjusted): 1995M03 2016M12
Included observations: 262 after adjustments
INFLATION = C(1)*INFLATION(-1) + C(2)*INFLATION(-2) + C(3)
    *UNEMPLOYMENT(-1) + C(4)*UNEMPLOYMENT(-2) + C(5)

	Coefficient	Std. Error	t-Statistic	Prob.
C(1)	0.726082	0.060971	11.90874	0.0000
C(2)	0.206498	0.060407	3.418458	0.0007
C(3)	-1.067401	0.300553	-3.551452	0.0005
C(4)	0.963779	0.302818	3.182698	0.0016
C(5)	0.005655	0.002976	1.900307	0.0585

R-squared	0.950914	Mean dependent var	0.019701
Adjusted R-squared	0.950150	S.D. dependent var	0.035120
S.E. of regression	0.007841	Akaike info criterion	-6.839929
Sum squared resid	0.015802	Schwarz criterion	-6.771831
Log likelihood	901.0307	Hannan-Quinn criter.	-6.812559
F-statistic	1244.677	Durbin-Watson stat	2.004337
Prob(F-statistic)	0.000000		

Table 6.8 shows that there is a significant relationship between the inflation and unemployment according to the above model. Other than the constant all coefficients are significant at 5% of significance level which is an indication of the short term causality. It is identified from R-Square value that 95.09% of the dependent variable is explained by the model. Model is significant at the 5% of significance level as the F-

statistic is significant. Durbin Watson test statistic is close to 2 indicates that there is no serial correlation among the residuals.

Residual Tests for the model 1

It is necessary to conduct residual test to confirm the accuracy of the model. Three Assumptions are made on the error term of the model 1. Residuals are Random. 2. Residuals are normally distributed. 3. Residuals are not serially correlated

Residuals are Random

Figure 6.7 correlogram of squared residuals under Null Hypothesis of Residuals are random shows that not at all cases the residuals are not random. Therefore it is concluded that the residuals are random.

Autocorrelation	Partial Correlation		AC	PAC	Q-Stat	Prob
		1	0.178	0.178	8.4337	0.004
		2	-0.018	-0.051	8.5193	0.014
		3	-0.041	-0.029	8.9624	0.030
		4	-0.003	0.009	8.9647	0.062
		5	0.024	0.021	9.1171	0.104
		6	0.052	0.044	9.8498	0.131
		7	0.089	0.076	11.992	0.101
		8	-0.037	-0.065	12.361	0.136
		9	-0.018	0.009	12.448	0.189
		10	-0.009	-0.005	12.471	0.255
		11	0.055	0.054	13.314	0.273
		12	0.312	0.301	40.176	0.000

Figure 6.7 Correlogram of squared residuals

Normality of the Residuals

Jarque-Bera Test statistic is tests under the Null Hypothesis of Errors are distributed normally can be used to test the normality of the residuals.

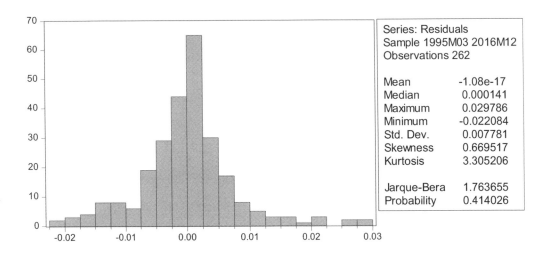

Figure 6.8 : Normality test for the residuals

According to the figure 6.8 P-value of Jarque Bera test statistic is not significant at 5% of significance level. Therefore it can be concluded that Residuals are normally distributed.

Serial Correlation Of The Residuals

Breusch-Godfrey Serial Correlation LM Test under Null Hypothesis of No Serial Correlation of the residuals can be used to test the serial correlation of the residuals.

Table 6.9 Breusch-Godfrey Serial Correlation LM Test

F-statistic	0.052292	Prob. F(2,255)	0.9491
Obs*R-squared	0.107411	Prob. Chi-Square(2)	0.9477

Test Equation:
Dependent Variable: RESID
Method: Least Squares
Sample: 1995M03 2016M12

Presample missing value lagged residuals set to zero.

Variable	Coefficient	Std. Error	t-Statistic	Prob.
C(1)	0.010462	0.369887	0.028285	0.9775
C(2)	-0.006767	0.348395	-0.019424	0.9845
C(3)	-0.008210	0.358604	-0.022894	0.9818
C(4)	0.014814	0.345730	0.042848	0.9659
C(5)	-0.000367	0.003681	-0.099626	0.9207
RESID(-1)	-0.014815	0.371813	-0.039844	0.9682
RESID(-2)	-0.019230	0.103166	-0.186401	0.8523
R-squared	0.000410	Mean dependent var		-1.08E-17
Adjusted R-squared	-0.023110	S.D. dependent var		0.007781
S.E. of regression	0.007870	Akaike info criterion		-6.825072
Sum squared resid	0.015795	Schwarz criterion		-6.729735
Log likelihood	901.0845	Hannan-Quinn criter.		-6.786754
F-statistic	0.017431	Durbin-Watson stat		2.000082
Prob(F-statistic)	0.999977			

According to the table 6.9 Null Hypothesis doesn't get rejected as the p-value is not significant. Therefore it can be concluded that the residuals are not serially correlated.

Testing MODEL 2

Model 2 identifies the Unemployment as the forecasting variable and inflation is calculated using first ,second lagged series of unemployment and inflation.

unemployment = - 0.0172*inflation(-1) + 0.0141*inflation(-2) + 1.5716*unemployment(-1) - 0.5867*unemployment(-2) + 0.0007

Significance of the model 2

Table 6.10 : Testing the significance of the model

Dependent Variable: UNEMPLOYMENT
Method: Least Squares
Sample (adjusted): 1995M03 2016M12
Included observations: 262 after adjustments
UNEMPLOYMENT = C(6)*INFLATION(-1) + C(7)*INFLATION(-2) + C(8)
*UNEMPLOYMENT(-1) + C(9)*UNEMPLOYMENT(-2) + C(10)

	Coefficient	Std. Error	t-Statistic	Prob.
C(6)	-0.017193	0.010198	-1.685863	0.0930
C(7)	0.014063	0.010104	1.391800	0.1652
C(8)	1.571636	0.050272	31.26265	0.0000
C(9)	-0.586717	0.050651	-11.58355	0.0000
C(10)	0.000744	0.000498	1.495357	0.1360

R-squared	0.992950	Mean dependent var	0.044916
Adjusted R-squared	0.992840	S.D. dependent var	0.015500
S.E. of regression	0.001312	Akaike info criterion	-10.41628
Sum squared resid	0.000442	Schwarz criterion	-10.34819
Log likelihood	1369.533	Hannan-Quinn criter.	-10.38891
F-statistic	9048.868	Durbin-Watson stat	2.184376
Prob(F-statistic)	0.000000		

According to the table 6.10 it can be seen that only coefficient of C(8) and C(9) are significant at 5% of significance level. It is identified from R-Square value that 99.29% of the dependent variable is explained by the model. Model is significant at the 5% of significance level as the F-statistic is significant. Durbin Watson test statistic is close to 2 indicates that there is no serial correlation among the residuals.

Residual Tests for the Model 2
It is necessary to conduct residual test to confirm the accuracy of the model. Three Assumptions on the Residuals of the model should be tested

Residuals Are Random
Figure 6.9 correlogram of squared residuals under Null Hypothesis of Residuals are random shows that at almost all cases the residuals are random. Therefore it is concluded that the residuals are random.

Autocorrelation	Partial Correlation		AC	PAC	Q-Stat	Prob
		1	0.154	0.154	6.3188	0.012
		2	0.105	0.083	9.2395	0.010
		3	0.022	-0.006	9.3637	0.025
		4	0.026	0.015	9.5412	0.049
		5	0.051	0.046	10.245	0.069
		6	0.028	0.011	10.452	0.107
		7	0.110	0.099	13.718	0.056
		8	-0.074	-0.111	15.207	0.055
		9	-0.040	-0.035	15.646	0.075
		10	0.040	0.068	16.078	0.097
		11	0.027	0.015	16.275	0.131
		12	0.069	0.049	17.585	0.129

Figure 6.9: Correlogram of squared residuals

Normality Of The Residuals

Jarque-Bera Test statistic is tests under the Null Hypothesis of residuals are distributed normally can be used to test the normality of the residuals.

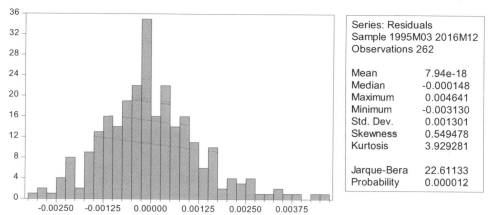

Figure 6.10: Normality test for the residuals

According to the figure 6.10 P-value of Jarque-Bera test statistic is significant at 5% of significance level. Therefore it can be concluded that Residuals are not normally distributed.

Serial Correlation Of The Residuals

Breusch-Godfrey Serial Correlation LM Test under Null Hypothesis of No Serial Correlation of the residuals can be used to test the serial correlation of the residuals.

Table 6.10 Breusch-Godfrey Serial Correlation LM Test

Breusch-Godfrey Serial Correlation LM Test:			
F-statistic	3.428987	Prob. F(2,255)	0.0339
Obs*R-squared	6.861693	Prob. Chi-Square(2)	0.0324

Test Equation:
Dependent Variable: RESID
Method: Least Squares
Date: 07/21/18   Time: 22:35
Sample: 1995M03 2016M12
Included observations: 262

Presample missing value lagged residuals set to zero.

Variable	Coefficient	Std. Error	t-Statistic	Prob.
C(6)	0.001299	0.010118	0.128410	0.8979
C(7)	-0.001176	0.010035	-0.117209	0.9068
C(8)	0.247729	0.130876	1.892857	0.0595
C(9)	-0.244804	0.129099	-1.896242	0.0591
C(10)	-0.000144	0.000506	-0.284473	0.7763
RESID(-1)	-0.347407	0.151105	-2.299111	0.0223
RESID(-2)	-0.084612	0.100428	-0.842520	0.4003

R-squared	0.026190	Mean dependent var	7.94E-18
Adjusted R-squared	0.003276	S.D. dependent var	0.001301
S.E. of regression	0.001299	Akaike info criterion	-10.42756
Sum squared resid	0.000431	Schwarz criterion	-10.33222
Log likelihood	1373.010	Hannan-Quinn criter.	-10.38924
F-statistic	1.142996	Durbin-Watson stat	2.014031
Prob(F-statistic)	0.337796		

According to the table 6.10 Null Hypothesis get rejected as the p-value is significant at 5% significance level. Therefore it can be concluded that the residuals are serially correlated.

Due to violation of two assumptions on Residuals, model two is not taken for further consideration. It is decided to use model 1 of "inflation = 0.7261*inflation(-1) + 0.2065*inflation(-2) - 1.0674*unemployment(-1) + 0.9638* unemployment(-2) + 0.00566 " for further studies.

Validation of the VAR (2) Model 1

Model 1 is identified as a suitable model for further studies.

Future forecast has been done from January 2017 to December 2017 for the below model using e-views software. They are recorded as the predicted value in Table 6.11.

Model:

inflation = 0.7261*inflation(-1) + 0.2065*inflation(-2) - 1.0674*unemployment(-1) + 0.9638*unemployment(-2) + 0.0057

Table 6.11. Percentage Error for the VAR model 1

Time	Observed value	Predicted value	Percentage error
Jan-17	0.0127	0.01884	32.59023
Feb-17	-0.0010	0.01881	105.3163
Mar-17	0.0050	0.01879	73.3901
Apr-17	0.0205	0.01876	9.275053
May-17	0.0196	0.01874	4.589114
Jun-17	0.0196	0.01872	4.700855
Jul-17	0.0195	0.01869	4.333868
Aug-17	0.0195	0.01867	4.445635
Sep-17	0.0145	0.01865	22.25201
Oct-17	0.0155	0.01863	16.80086
Nov-17	0.0154	0.01861	17.24879
Dec-17	0.0173	0.01859	6.939215

Table 6.11 shows that percentage error is fairly low. Most of calculated percentage error lies between + 10%.

6.4   Short Run and Long Run causality

Tests on Short term and long term causality are important to find out if there is a long term or short term effect from one time series model to other time series model

Short Term Causality

Granger Causality Test is used to identify the short run causality in variables. Under the null hypothesis of Unemployment does not granger cause inflation Granger causality for inflation is tested.

Table 6.12 VAR Granger Causality/Block Exogeneity Wald Tests

Dependent variable: INFLATION			
Excluded	Chi-sq	df	Prob.
UNEMPLOYMENT	15.39181	2	0.0005
All	15.39181	2	0.0005

According to table 6.12 it can be observed that unemployment granger cause inflation at 5% of confidence level. It can be concluded that there is short term causality running from Unemployment to Inflation. Unemployment rate has short term effect on Inflation rate which again confirms the conditions of the Phillips curve.

Long Term Causality

Long run causality is checked by co-integration test. As mentioned earlier Co-Integration Test there is no co-integration founded in this VAR model. Therefore it can be concluded that there is no Long run causality happens either from Unemployment to Inflation or inflation to Unemployment.

6.5   Impulse Responses

Impulse response is the reaction of a system as a function of the time. They shows the nature of response to shocks.

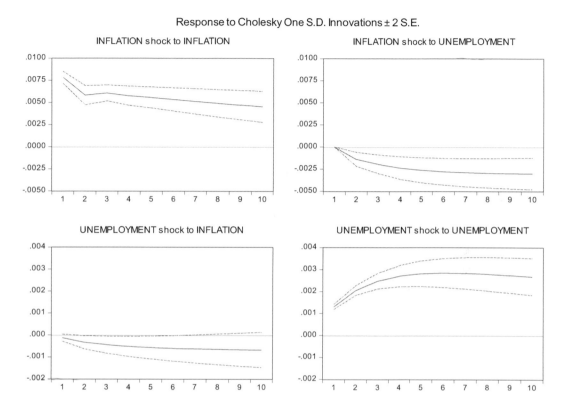

Figure 6.11 Impulse response functions

Figure 6.11 shows the shocks of variables on other variable or on its own with 95% of confidence interval. Inflation and Unemployment has inverse relationship in shocks.

Figure 6.12 :Relationship of Unemployment and Inflation according to the selected VAR(2) Model

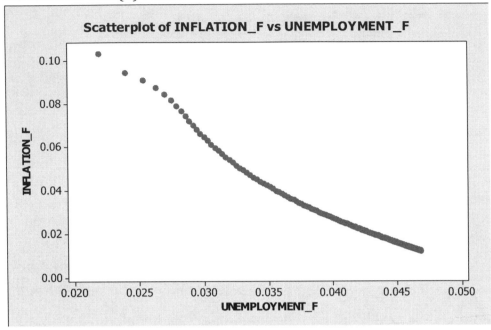

Figure 6.12 has been plotted using the model of "inflation = 0.7261*inflation(-1) + 0.2065*inflation(-2) - 1.0674*unemployment(-1) + 0.9638* unemployment(-2) + 0.0057 "

Scatter plot shows a inverse relationship between inflation rate and unemployment rate. It takes a similar shape to Phillips Curve.

Conclusion

No co-integration has been identified between two time series , therefore no long run relationship exist between unemployment rate and inflation rate of Hong Kong. The finding of VAR model , granger causality test indicates the presence of short run impact of unemployment rate on the inflation rate. The study supports the fact of the existence of the Phillips Curve in the context of Chinese Special Administrative Region of Hong Kong which is considered as one of the Tigers in Asian Economy.

6.6 Vector Error Correction Model Estimation

Example 6.2 : VECM

Now we are going to apply a vector error correction model for the data given in datasheet. Check for VECM data sheet in excel sheet,

Table : List of the variables used for the study

Notation	Stands For	Description	Units
INF	Inflation Rate	Quarterly inflation rate calculated	Percentage Value
GDP	Gross Domestic Product	Real Gross Domestic Product, Quarterly, Seasonally Adjusted Annual Rate	Billions of US Dollars
TOB	Trade of Balance	Trade of Balance	Millions of US Dollars
EXC	Exchange Rate	Real Effective Exchange Rate, based on Consumer Price Index	Percentage Value
MS	Money Supply	M2 Money Supply	Billions of US Dollars
FDI	Foreign Direct Investment	Rest of the world; foreign direct investment in U.S.A.; asset, Flow, Quarterly, Seasonally Adjusted Annual Rate	Millions of US Dollars
GE	Government Expenditures	Federal government total expenditures, Quarterly, Seasonally Adjusted Annual Rate	Billions of US Dollars
UMP	Unemployment Rate	Percentage of unemployment rate quarterly	Percentage Value

Table 6. Descriptive Statistics

	INF	EXC	FDI	GDP
Mean	0.03	107.38	141980.80	11408.41
Median	0.03	105.13	82306.00	11248.40
Maximum	0.04	121.21	562804.00	13260.51
Minimum	0.01	96.08	23068.00	9850.97
Std. Dev.	0.01	6.85	137223.00	1075.13
Skewness	-0.50	0.32	1.64	0.26
Kurtosis	2.28	1.79	4.75	1.80
Jarque-Bera	2.02	2.49	18.51	2.28
Probability	0.36	0.29	0.00	0.32
Sum	0.83	3436.30	4543384.00	365069.20
Sum Sq. Dev.	0.00	1452.61	584000000000.00	35832822.00
Observations	32	32	32	32

	GE	MS	TOB	UMP
Mean	972.35	3975800.00	55375.92	5.31
Median	962.20	3853600.00	45884.15	5.23
Maximum	1306.22	4945500.00	120833.10	7.73
Minimum	656.94	3414800.00	20904.60	3.77
Std. Dev.	198.42	486853.40	27165.63	1.04
Skewness	0.14	0.55	1.06	0.49
Kurtosis	1.79	1.92	3.03	2.40
Jarque-Bera	2.07	3.15	6.03	1.76
Probability	0.36	0.21	0.05	0.41
Sum	31115.21	127000000.00	1772029.00	170.07
Sum Sq. Dev.	1220460.00	7350000000000	22900000000.00	33.82
Observations	32	32	32	32

VAR Model Estimation
Stationary of Time Series Variables
Stationary of the variables should be identified before applying any time series model. Augmented Dicky Fuller Test (ADF) and P-Perron (PP) test can be used to identify the stationary of the economical time series effectively.

Table 6.14: Probability Values of Unit Root Test results of Sequence of level

Variable	Level		First Difference	
	ADF	PP	ADF	PP
LNINF	0.0256	0.4006	0.0742	0.0024
LNEXC	0.9635	0.9635	0.0001	0.0001
LNFDI	0.7476	0.2614	0.0000	0.0001
LNGDP	0.9902	0.9930	0.0000	0.0000
LNGE	0.6498	0.0173	0.0047	0.0000
LNMS	0.9554	1.0000	0.6001	0.0048
LNTOB	0.9952	0.7369	0.4174	0.0000
LNUMP	0.8082	0.5915	0.1752	0.0001

As indicated in table 6.14 ADF test and PP tests show that all variables become stationary by applying first difference as all p-values are less than 5%.

Lag Length Criteria
Identifying a suitable lag length is important before applying VEC model. According to the table 6.15 the suitable lag length for the given economical variables is lag order 1 as selected by Akaike Information Criterea , Shwartz Baysian and Hannan Quinn (HQ). (* indicates lag order selected by the criterion)

Table 6.15: Determine Lag Intervals with VAR Lag order selection criteria for 8 economic variables

VAR Lag Order Selection Criteria Endogenous variables: LNINF LNEXC LNFDI LNGDP LNGE LNMS LNTOB LNUMP Exogenous variables: C Sample: 1993Q1 2000Q4 Included observations: 31						
Lag	LogL	LR	FPE	AIC	SC	HQ
0	337.0990	NA	8.30e-20	-21.23219	-20.86213	-21.11156
1	583.4546	349.6660*	7.40e-25*	-32.99707*	-29.66652*	-31.91140*
* indicates lag order selected by the criterion LR: sequential modified LR test statistic (each test at 5% level) FPE: Final prediction error AIC: Akaike information criterion SC: Schwarz information criterion HQ: Hannan-Quinn information criterion						

Co-integration of the Time Series Variables

VEC models are used for I(1) variables. Presence of co-integration indicates non stationary variables. Johansen Co-integration test is used to identify the existence of the co-integration. As indicated in table 6.16 there exists co-integration between endogenous variables. VEC model should be applied for the time series data.

Table 6.16: Johansen Co-integration test for 8 economic variables

Sample: 1993Q1 2000Q4
Included observations: 30
Series: LNINF LNEXC LNFDI LNGDP LNGE LNMS LNTOB LNUMP
Lags interval: 1 to 1
    Selected (0.05 level*) Number of Cointegrating Relations by Model

Data Trend:	None	None	Linear	Linear	Quadratic
Test Type	No Intercept No Trend	Intercept No Trend	Intercept No Trend	Intercept Trend	Intercept Trend
Trace	6	7	7	8	5
Max-Eig	4	3	2	3	3

*Critical values based on MacKinnon-Haug-Michelis (1999)

VEC Model

Table 6.17 shows the VEC model estimated using lag order 1. The t-statistics shown in the squared brackets should be greater than 2.0 for lag order to be significant. Inflation rate is taken as the endogenous variable and other nine variables as the exogenous variables. Using VEC model long term error correction among the variables has been identified.

Table 6.17: VEC Model for selected economic variables in U.S.A

Vector Error Correction Estimates
Sample (adjusted): 1993Q3 2000Q4
Included observations: 30 after adjustments
Standard errors in ( ) & t-statistics in [ ]

Cointegrating Eq:	CointEq1
LNINF(-1)	1.000000
LNEXC(-1)	-0.080068
	(0.34182)
	[-0.23424]
LNFDI(-1)	-0.090865
	(0.02928)
	[-3.10379]
LNGDP(-1)	-3.265895
	(2.28566)
	[-1.42887]

152

LNGE(-1)	-2.374673	
	(0.59820)	
	[-3.96969]	
LNMS(-1)	5.363180	
	(0.84257)	
	[6.36526]	
LNTOB(-1)	-1.268402	
	(0.07336)	
	[-17.2907]	
LNUMP(-1)	-4.519676	
	(0.24961)	
	[-18.1068]	
C	-8.867394	

Error Correction:	D(LNINF)	D(LNEXC)	D(LNFDI)	D(LNGDP)	D(LNGE)	D(LNMS)	D(LNTOB)	D(LNUMP)
CointEq1	-0.005425	-0.021588	0.002931	0.008294	0.010011	0.001634	0.672129	0.356238
	(0.09943)	(0.02580)	(0.71130)	(0.00682)	(0.02448)	(0.00993)	(0.14310)	(0.03498)
	[-0.05457]	[-0.83686]	[0.00412]	[1.21589]	[0.40900]	[0.16457]	[4.69677]	[10.1827]
D(LNINF(-1))	0.418058	-0.022298	0.902292	-0.002504	-0.018503	0.012529	-0.437760	-0.186691
	(0.23516)	(0.06101)	(1.68230)	(0.01613)	(0.05789)	(0.02348)	(0.33846)	(0.08274)
	[1.77778]	[-0.36547]	[0.53634]	[-0.15523]	[-0.31961]	[0.53363]	[-1.29340]	[-2.25628]
D(LNEXC(-1))	0.095131	0.185499	2.495829	0.020341	-0.050782	0.130414	-2.183144	-0.225420
	(0.82939)	(0.21519)	(5.93338)	(0.05690)	(0.20418)	(0.08281)	(1.19372)	(0.29183)
	[0.11470]	[0.86203]	[0.42064]	[0.35747]	[-0.24871]	[1.57483]	[-1.82885]	[-0.77244]
D(LNFDI(-1))	-0.026533	-0.004315	-0.544093	0.001578	0.001640	-0.000680	0.014000	0.020419
	(0.02988)	(0.00775)	(0.21379)	(0.00205)	(0.00736)	(0.00298)	(0.04301)	(0.01052)
	[-0.88786]	[-0.55648]	[-2.54496]	[0.76971]	[0.22296]	[-0.22786]	[0.32550]	[1.94184]
D(LNGDP(-1))	6.912856	-2.124134	-18.15603	0.083223	0.063532	0.081836	10.96206	2.114968
	(4.04950)	(1.05065)	(28.9697)	(0.27782)	(0.99691)	(0.40432)	(5.82835)	(1.42486)
	[1.70709]	[-2.02173]	[-0.62672]	[0.29955]	[0.06373]	[0.20240]	[1.88082]	[1.48434]
D(LNGE(-1))	-0.538005	-0.101845	-0.224245	0.021477	-0.451680	-0.201957	1.064596	0.225627
	(0.74744)	(0.19392)	(5.34711)	(0.05128)	(0.18400)	(0.07463)	(1.07577)	(0.26299)
	[-0.71980]	[-0.52518]	[-0.04194]	[0.41882]	[-2.45472]	[-2.70617]	[0.98961]	[0.85792]

D(LNMS(-1))	-0.240979	1.670967	11.14475	-0.031311	-0.403498	0.524567	-7.695026	-2.696004
	(1.91600)	(0.49711)	(13.7069)	(0.13145)	(0.47168)	(0.19130)	(2.75765)	(0.67416)
	[-0.12577]	[3.36136]	[0.81308]	[0.23820]	[0.85545]	[2.74206]	[2.79043]	[-3.99904]
D(LNTOB(-1))	-0.011937	-0.005184	1.821381	0.013112	-0.005583	0.029812	0.623654	0.260166
	(0.13357)	(0.03465)	(0.95552)	(0.00916)	(0.03288)	(0.01334)	(0.19224)	(0.04700)
	[-0.08937]	[0.14958]	[1.90617]	[1.43084]	[0.16979]	[2.23548]	[3.24416]	[5.53585]
D(LNUMP(-1))	0.001860	0.044947	-0.921423	-0.002585	-0.007630	0.002496	1.813581	-0.167435
	(0.17754)	(0.04606)	(1.27012)	(0.01218)	(0.04371)	(0.01773)	(0.25553)	(0.06247)
	[0.01048]	[0.97575]	[0.72546]	[0.21222]	[0.17458]	[0.14081]	[7.09728]	[-2.68025]
C	-0.048749	0.010346	0.028231	0.007766	0.035581	0.007544	0.016290	-0.034913
	(0.04364)	(0.01132)	(0.31221)	(0.00299)	(0.01074)	(0.00436)	(0.06281)	(0.01536)
	[-1.11702]	[0.91375]	[0.09042]	[2.59368]	[3.31178]	[1.73117]	[0.25935]	[-2.27360]

R-squared	0.299673	0.430323	0.625036	0.197113	0.341188	0.576487	0.799902	0.959518
Adj. R-squared	-0.015475	0.173968	0.456303	-0.164187	0.044723	0.385906	0.709858	0.941300
Sum sq. resids	0.100161	0.006742	5.126070	0.000471	0.006070	0.000999	0.207485	0.012400
S.E. equation	0.070767	0.018361	0.506264	0.004855	0.017422	0.007066	0.101854	0.024900
F-statistic	0.950897	1.678624	3.704280	0.545566	1.150855	3.024897	8.883456	52.67126
Log likelihood	42.96448	83.43994	-16.06528	123.3454	85.01523	112.0884	32.04025	74.30013
Akaike AIC	-2.197632	-4.895996	1.737686	-7.556357	-5.001015	-6.805890	-1.469350	-4.286676
Schwarz SC	-1.730566	-4.428930	2.204751	-7.089291	-4.533950	-6.338824	-1.002284	-3.819610
Mean dependent	0.001901	0.005965	0.071538	0.009714	0.021053	0.012063	0.048998	-0.021698
S.D. dependent	0.070226	0.020202	0.686592	0.004500	0.017825	0.009017	0.189092	0.102775

Determinant resid covariance (dof adj.)	4.50E-26
Determinant resid covariance	1.76E-27
Log likelihood	583.5438
Akaike information criterion	-33.03625
Schwarz criterion	-28.92607

Although Table 6.17 shows the whole output of the vector error correction model, it can be summarized according to table 6.18 when presenting it in a research paper.

Table 6.18 : Summary of Vector Error Correction Model Results
Long Run Equation (Period 2)

Variable	Coefficient
Speed of Adjustment	-8.867394(Long Run)
LNEXC(-1)	-0.080068
	[-0.23424]
LNFDI(-1)	-0.090865
	[-3.10379]
LNGDP(-1)	-3.265895
	[-1.42887]
LNGE(-1)	-2.374673
	[-3.96969]
LNMS(-1)	5.363180
	[6.36526]
LNTOB(-1)	-1.268402
	[-17.2907]
LNUMP(-1)	-4.519676
	[-18.1068]

Source: Author's computation using E-View version 10

Table 6.18 shows the VEC model estimated using lag order 1. The t-statistics shown in the squared brackets should be greater than 2.0 for lag order to be significant. Inflation rate is taken as the endogenous variable and other seven variables as the exogenous variables.

Below equation of VEC model 2 can be derived from the table 6.18 and it can be used to check the significance of the coefficients as shown in table 6.18.

$LNINF_t = 8.8674 - 0.0801*LNEXC_{t-1} - 0.09087*LNFDI_{t-1} - 3.2659*LNGDP_{t-1} - 2.3747*LNGE_{t-1} + 5.3632*LNMS_{t-1} - 1.2684*LNTOB_{t-1} - 4.5197*LNUMP_{t-1}$

As shown in table 6.19, significance of coefficients will be identified at 5% of significance level in order to confirm the effect on inflation rate.

Table 6.19: Properties of the coefficient of the VEC model

Dependent Variable: D(LNINF)
Method: Least Squares
Sample (adjusted): 1993Q3 2000Q4
Included observations: 30 after adjustments

D(LNINF) = C(1)*(LNINF(-1) - 0.0800679792647*LNEXC(-1) -
    0.0908653828276*LNFDI(-1) - 3.26589511482*LNGDP(-1) -
    2.37467305011*LNGE(-1) + 5.36318035659*LNMS(-1) -
    1.26840178669*LNTOB(-1) - 4.51967568795*LNUMP(-1) -
    8.86739360747) + C(2)*D(LNINF(-1)) + C(3)*D(LNEXC(-1)) + C(4)
    *D(LNFDI(-1)) + C(5)*D(LNGDP(-1)) + C(6)*D(LNGE(-1)) + C(7)
    *D(LNMS(-1)) + C(8)*D(LNTOB(-1)) + C(9)*D(LNUMP(-1)) + C(10)

	Coefficient	Std. Error	t-Statistic	Prob.
C(1)	-0.005425	0.099428	-0.054565	0.9570
C(2)	0.418058	0.235158	1.777776	0.0907
C(3)	0.095131	0.829390	0.114700	0.9098
C(4)	-0.026533	0.029885	-0.887858	0.3852
C(5)	6.912856	4.049495	1.707091	0.1033
C(6)	-0.538005	0.747439	-0.719798	0.4800
C(7)	-0.240979	1.915998	-0.125772	0.9012
C(8)	-0.011937	0.133566	-0.089374	0.9297
C(9)	0.001860	0.177542	0.010475	0.9917
C(10)	-0.048749	0.043642	-1.117018	0.2772

R-squared	0.299673	Mean dependent var	0.001901
Adjusted R-squared	-0.015475	S.D. dependent var	0.070226
S.E. of regression	0.070767	Akaike info criterion	-2.197632
Sum squared resid	0.100161	Schwarz criterion	-1.730566
Log likelihood	42.96448	Hannan-Quinn criter.	-2.048214
F-statistic	0.950897	Durbin-Watson stat	2.165755
Prob(F-statistic)	0.505703		

One lagged inflation rate, foreign direct investment, gross domestic product, money supply, exchange rate and unemployment rate have significant negative effect on inflation rate. One lagged government expenditure and trade of balance has a significant positive relationship to inflation rate as in table 6.19.

Residual Tests for VEC Model

Residual tests are done to confirm the validity of the model created. Table 5.20 shows the test results of portmanteau test for autocorrelation under the null hypothesis of no residual autocorrelations up to lag h proves that there is no autocorrelation among the lags at 5% of significant level.

Table 6.20: Portmanteau Test for Autocorrelation for VEC Model

VEC Residual Portmanteau Tests for Autocorrelations					
Null Hypothesis: no residual autocorrelations up to lag h					
Sample: 1993Q1 2000Q4					
Included observations: 30					
Lags	Q-Stat	Prob.	Adj Q-Stat	Prob.	df
1	36.79504	NA*	38.06384	NA*	NA*
2	114.1872	0.6324	120.9840	0.4576	120
3	162.2172	0.8746	174.3506	0.6834	184
4	241.2799	0.6082	265.5769	0.2115	248
5	290.2842	0.8061	324.3820	0.3030	312
6	350.5217	0.8229	399.6789	0.1921	376
7	405.2193	0.8814	471.0236	0.1481	440
8	460.1756	0.9194	545.9640	0.0955	504
9	501.7604	0.9787	605.3708	0.1346	568
10	552.5955	0.9897	681.6236	0.0839	632
11	590.8349	0.9984	742.0015	0.1104	696
12	643.3056	0.9992	829.4526	0.0403	760
*The test is valid only for lags larger than the VAR lag order.					
df is degrees of freedom for (approximate) chi-square distribution					

Null hypothesis of no serial correlation at lag order 12 is tested in table 6.21; it confirms that the hypothesis is significant at 5% of significant level. There is no serial correlation among the lags.

Table 6.21: Serial Correlation LM Test for VEC Model 2

VEC Residual Serial Correlation LM Tests
Null Hypothesis: no serial correlation at lag order h
Sample: 1993Q1 2000Q4
Included observations: 30

Lags	LM-Stat	Prob
1	75.69379	0.1504
2	76.92441	0.1289
3	32.86307	0.9996
4	91.19983	0.0144
5	53.37330	0.8257
6	68.53147	0.3263
7	63.13378	0.5071
8	64.23180	0.4684
9	70.72427	0.2633
10	57.31647	0.7099
11	52.45635	0.8483
12	70.97881	0.2565

Probs from chi-square with 64 df.

Table 6.22: Normality Tests for VEC Model

VEC Residual Normality Tests
Orthogonalization: Cholesky (Lutkepohl)
Null Hypothesis: residuals are multivariate normal
Sample: 1993Q1 2000Q4
Included observations: 30

Component	Jarque-Bera	df	Prob.
1	1.684313	2	0.4308
2	21.74035	2	0.0000
3	0.555336	2	0.7575
4	1.532379	2	0.4648
5	2.296769	2	0.3171
6	0.198741	2	0.9054
7	0.078498	2	0.9615
8	1.752877	2	0.4163
Joint	29.83926	16	0.0189

Jarque –Bera test statistic under the null hypothesis of residuals are multivariate normal is shown in table 6.22. Statistics of skewness and kurtosis supports the above indication.

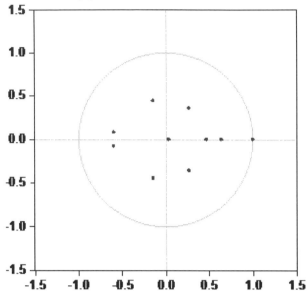

Figure 6.3: Inverse Roots of AR Stability of the VEC model 2

A causal invertible model should have all the roots outside the unit circle. Equivalently, the inverse roots should like inside the unit circle. If all roots have modulus less than one and lie inside the unit circle, then the estimated ARMA is stable (stationary) and invertible and therefore will give good estimates.

Stability of the variables can be identified using the AR root graph. Unit root graph in figure 6.3 confirms that there is no root outside the unit circle and VAR satisfies the stability condition. If there is dots outside the circle it is an indication of presence of unit root.

Granger Causality Test

There is no granger causality running among all variables to inflation rate during the period which confirms there is no short term causality running among variables as explained in table 6.23.

Table 6.23: Granger Causality Test

Null Hypothesis:	Obs	F-Statistic	Prob.	Decision
LNEXC does not Granger Cause LNINF	31	1.47076	0.2354	Do not Reject
LNINF does not Granger Cause LNEXC		0.37257	0.5465	Do not Reject
LNFDI does not Granger Cause LNINF	31	0.94169	0.3402	Do not Reject
LNINF does not Granger Cause LNFDI		0.27560	0.6037	Do not Reject
LNGDP does not Granger Cause LNINF	31	2.15322	0.1534	Do not Reject
LNINF does not Granger Cause LNGDP		1.34713	0.2556	Do not Reject
LNGE does not Granger Cause LNINF	31	1.26751	0.2698	Do not Reject
LNINF does not Granger Cause LNGE		1.0E-05	0.9975	Do not Reject
LNMS does not Granger Cause LNINF	31	2.44156	0.1294	Do not Reject
LNINF does not Granger Cause LNMS		0.75557	0.3921	Do not Reject
LNTOB does not Granger Cause LNINF	31	3.20147	0.0844	Do not Reject
LNINF does not Granger Cause LNTOB		0.35110	0.5582	Do not Reject
LNUMP does not Granger Cause LNINF	31	1.49841	0.2311	Do not Reject
LNINF does not Granger Cause LNUMP		0.61254	0.4404	Do not Reject

Impulse Responses Functions

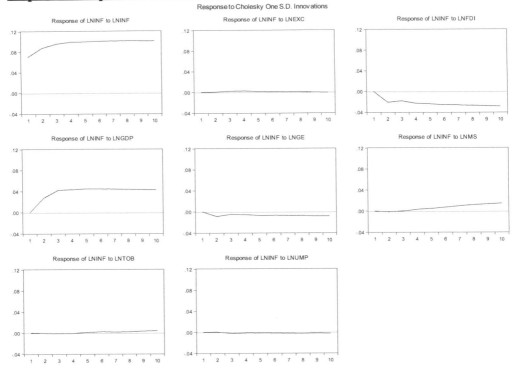

Figure 6.4: Impulse Responses Functions

Impulse responses at figure 6.4 shows that there is a positive response of inflation to the shock of inflation rate , exchange rate , gross domestic product money supply and trade of balance . There is a negative response of inflation to the shock of foreign direct investment government expenditure and unemployment rate.

Period	Significant Variables
1993Q1-2000Q4	$LNINF_{t-1}$, $LNEXC_{t-1}$, $LNFDI_{t-1}$, $LNGDP_{t-1}$, $LNGE_{t-1}$, $LNMS_{t-1}$, $LNTOB_{t-1}$, $LNUMP_{t-1}$

Period	Positively influenced	Negatively influenced
1993Q1-2000Q4	$LNINF_{t-1}$, $LNMS_{t-1}$, $LNTOB_{t-1}$	$LNEXC_{t-1}$, $LNFDI_{t-1}$, $LNGDP_{t-1}$, $LNGE_{t-1}$, $LNUMP_{t-1}$

During the second period (From 1993Q1 to 2000Q4) which is a democratic period one lagged inflation rate, one lagged money supply and one lagged balance of trade have a positive relationship with inflation rate while one lagged exchange rate, one lagged foreign direct investment, one lagged gross domestic product, one lagged government expenditure, and one lagged unemployment rate have a positive relationship with the inflation rate.

Chapter Seven:
Autoregressive Distributed Lag Model (ARDL)

7.1 Introduction
We can use the ARDL model when the relationship of multiple time series variables should be presented in one equation, in time series. This method helps us to identify if the underlying variables are co-integrated when given the endogenous variable/ dependent.

ARDL can be used regardless the underlying variables are co-integrated at the first difference, but none of the variables should be co-integrated in the second difference. When there are variables with a mixture of co integration at level I(0)and first difference I(1)We can use ARDL When there is one co-integrating vector as well. ARDL model proves to be more efficient in defining short-run and long-run relationships, when there is a few numbers of observations in a time series.
There is Linear ARDL models and Non-Linear ARDL (NADRL) models.

7.2 ARDL bound test

ARDL bound test is based on the assumption that the variables are I(0) or I(1). Variables shouldn't be I(2). If variables are I(2),we cannot interpret the values of statistics provided by Pesaran et el. Bound test which was developed by Pesaran et al in 2001 can be used to identify long term relationship among the integrated parameters. Long term relationship is identified by comparing Bound F test against upper and lower critical values provided for different significance levels. (In this book the preferred significance level for all statistical tests is 5%). If the F statistic is higher than critical value I (1) then there is a long run co-integration and the null hypothesis of "no co-integration among variables/no long run relationship among variables" is rejected. If the F statistic is lower than I (0) the model has lack of evidence to identify a long run relationship among the variables.

Advantages

1. It is not necessary for all the variables are integrated at the same level. It can be sued for the mix of I(0) and I(1).
2. Can apply for small and finite data size.
3. We can obtain unbiased estimated for long run model.

General ARDL model equation is as below :

$$y_t = B_0 x_t + B_1 x_{t-1} + B_2 x_{t-2} + \ldots + B_k x_{t-k} + e_t$$

y= Indegenous variable

x= exogenous variable

B= coefficients

t-k= lag

e = error

ARDL (1,1) Model which express both indigenous and exogenous in short run can be represented as below. (In short run y is considered to be stable).

$$y_t = a_0 + a_1 y_{t-1} + B_0 x_t + B_2 x_{t-1} + e_t \qquad \text{where } t = 1,2,\ldots t$$

y= Indegenous variable

x= exogenous variable

a= -1<a<1- the speed of adjustment towards the long run model

Long Run or the steady state of the ARDL model is expressed as below.

$$y_t = \frac{a_0}{1-a_1} + \left[\frac{B_0 - B_1}{1-a_1}\right] x_t + \left[\frac{e_t}{1-a_1}\right]$$

7.3   Error Correction Model

ARDL models can be re-parameterized to create an Error Correction Model, when co-integrating parameters are known. ARDL is an

Ordinary Least Square based model. Error Correction Model is calculated when there is a presence of long run relationship among variables. Error correction term represents the speed of adjustment of the model towards long run equilibrium. Error correction term should be a significant negative value which is less than 1. Value over 1 indicates a speed of adjustment over 100% which is not real in practical world.

Preconditions of applying ARDL Models should be satisfied before continuing further analysis. In previous chapter time series models are tested for stationary using Augmented Dicky Fuller test and Phillips Perron test. In order to apply ARDL model all variables in time series should be integrated at level I(0) or first difference I(1) as explained in previous chapters. But variables should not be integrated at second level I(2). Then proper number of lags is selected using an appropriate lag selection method.

The models should be tested for its stability and also residual diagnostic tests should be implemented.

If there is autocorrelation in errors then the model won't be consistent. , Breusch-Godfrey Serial Correlation LM is used to test the serial correlation of the model. Model should be free of heteroskedasticity , Breusch- Pagan Heteroskedasticity test is used to check the heteroskedasticity of the model. Stability of the models can be tested using cumulative sum (CUSUM) and cumulative sum of square (CUSUMQ). Stability tests shows if the model is stable over the time.

7.4   CUSUM Test

Cumulative sum (CUSUM) and CUSUM of squares (CUSUMSQ) tests are used for checking the structure stability in the model. If the residual series falls between the control limits, then the model is stable. These two test are used in quality control as well. Below graph shows the CUSUM test results for stable model. CUSUM test identify if the sequence value of the sequence of the model can be modeled as random. Cusum tests assess the stability of coefficients (β) in a multiple linear regression model of the form y = Xβ + ε.

CUSUM Test

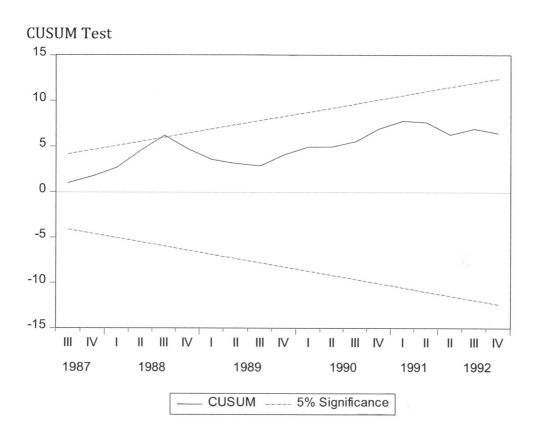

CUSUM Square Test

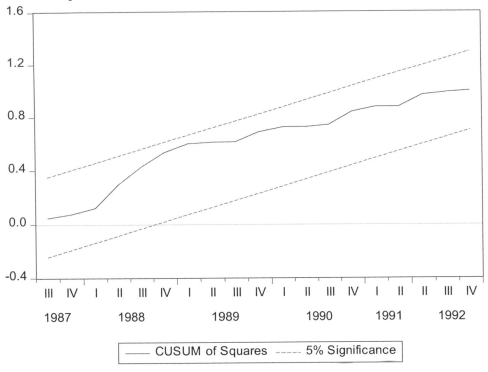

Example 7.1 :ARDL Model
The data can be found in the datasheet, Look for ARDL LOG data sheet in excel. Original data is in ARDL datasheet in excel file.

The variables are in different measures, therefore they should be transformed into log before analyzing data. After log transformation, use the correlation matrix to find the correlation of the economic variables.

Eviews steps : Open variables as Group> View > Covariance Analysis > Select Correlation and Probability

Table 7.1 Correlation Matrix Table

Covariance Probability	LNEXC	LNFDI	LNGDP	LNGE	LNINF	LNMS	LNTB	LNTOB	LNTX	LNUMP
LNEXC	0.017492									

LNFDI	-0.039200	0.506167								
	0.0032	-----								
LNGDP	-0.011047	0.046330	0.014467							
	0.0000	0.0001	-----							
LNGE	-0.021046	0.079428	0.023702	0.040617						
	0.0000	0.0000	0.0000	-----						
LNINF	-0.005176	-0.011083	-0.012911	-0.012489	0.096415					
	0.3933	0.7349	0.0161	0.1739	-----					
LNMS	-0.019064	0.081986	0.026939	0.043455	-0.032416	0.051822				
	0.0000	0.0002	0.0000	0.0000	0.0010	-----				
LNTB	0.021674	-0.045617	-0.032348	-0.049998	0.077500	-0.065539	0.128104			
	0.0011	0.2231	0.0000	0.0000	0.0000	0.0000	-----			
LNTOB	-0.000858	0.226011	0.041740	0.054646	-0.118316	0.084178	-0.113402	0.369945		
	0.9426	0.0001	0.0000	0.0015	0.0000	0.0000	0.0001	-----		
LNTX	-0.025911	0.104855	0.035424	0.057862	-0.036065	0.067124	-0.083223	0.103104	0.088644	
	0.0000	0.0003	0.0000	0.0000	0.0061	0.0000	0.0000	0.0000	-----	
LNUMP	0.015114	-0.103474	-0.017649	-0.030053	-0.002733	-0.030700	0.016631	-0.060905	-0.039815	0.039818
	0.0000	0.0000	0.0000	0.0000	0.7659	0.0000	0.1112	0.0003	0.0000	-----

Correlation matrix table shows that there is a significant individual linear relationship between inflation rate and other selected independent variables except Exchange Rate , Foreign Direct Investment, Government Expenditure and Unemployment. Further there are significant relationships between independent variables except combinations of (Unemployment rate , T-Bill rate).

Using Phillips Perron test for economic variables gives better results, and widely used in economic research. Therefore Phillips Perron test is used to test for the unit root of time series variables.

168

All variables are integrated at level I(0) or first difference I(1). In order to apply ARDL model variables should not be integrated at second level I(2). Neverthless ARDL model can be used if 92.5% of the variables are either I(1) or I(0). ARDL/ECM models are proven to be output accurate results for shorter time series. Results of unit root test are illustrated in below tables. (Table 7.2 table 7.3)You should install eviews 10 or higher to get ARDL model, otherwise ARDL should be estimated using LS. In this book we are using Eviews 11 software student version.

Eviews Steps : View> Unit Root Test > Individual Root Fisher –PP> Select level

Table 7.2 : Phillips Perron test results -Level of the selected economic variables

Null Hypothesis: Unit root (individual unit root process)
Series: LNEXC, LNFDI, LNGDP, LNGE, LNINF, LNMS,
    LNTB, LNTOB, LNTX, LNUMP
Sample: 1981Q1 1992Q4
Exogenous variables: Individual effects
Newey-West automatic bandwidth selection and Bartlett ke..
Total number of observations: 468
Cross-sections included: 10

Method	Statistic	Prob.**
PP - Fisher Chi-square	58.1074	0.0000
PP - Choi Z-stat	-1.78178	0.0374

** Probabilities for Fisher tests are computed using an
    asymptotic Chi-square distribution. All other tests
    assume asymptotic normality.

Intermediate Phillips-Perron test results UNTITLED

Series	Prob.	Bandwidth	Obs
LNEXC	0.7329	4.0	47
LNFDI	0.0191	3.0	45
LNGDP	0.9206	4.0	47
LNGE	0.9364	0.0	47
LNINF	0.0998	1.0	47
LNMS	0.0000	12.0	47
LNTB	0.8660	3.0	47
LNTOB	0.1155	5.0	47
LNTX	0.4895	6.0	47
LNUMP	0.4667	6.0	47

Eviews Steps : View> Unit Root Test > Individual Root Fisher –PP> Select 1st Difference

Table 7.3 : Phillips Perron test results –First Difference of the selected economic variables

Null Hypothesis: Unit root (individual unit root process)
Series: LNEXC, LNFDI, LNGDP, LNGE, LNINF, LNMS,
    LNTB, LNTOB, LNTX, LNUMP
Sample: 1981Q1 1992Q4
Exogenous variables: Individual effects
Newey-West automatic bandwidth selection and Bartlett ke...
Total number of observations: 457
Cross-sections included: 10

Method	Statistic	Prob.**
PP - Fisher Chi-square	279.995	0.0000
PP - Choi Z-stat	-14.5754	0.0000

** Probabilities for Fisher tests are computed using an
   asymptotic Chi-square distribution. All other tests
   assume asymptotic normality.

Intermediate Phillips-Perron test results D(UNTITLED)

Series	Prob.	Bandwidth	Obs
D(LNEXC)	0.0002	2.0	46
D(LNFDI)	0.0000	3.0	43
D(LNGDP)	0.0022	3.0	46
D(LNGE)	0.0000	3.0	46
D(LNINF)	0.0002	1.0	46
D(LNMS)	0.0008	1.0	46
D(LNTB)	0.0006	0.0	46
D(LNTOB)	0.0000	12.0	46
D(LNTX)	0.0000	4.0	46
D(LNUMP)	0.0000	4.0	46

The null hypothesis is "data series is not stationary". It get rejected at level and first difference tests. Therefore all variables are integrated at level I(0) or first difference I(1).

Calculating ARDL Model

After identifying the integration of the time series, next step should be identifying the lag length criteria of the time series. Lag selection is done through execution of vector auto-regression (VAR) in eviews. Five lag selection criteria uses here is Hanna Quinn Information Criterion, Akaike Information Criterion and Schwartz Information Criterion, FPE and LR.

170

Eviews Steps : Close all windows > Open all variables as VAR mode > View> Lag Structure > Lag length criteria (4 lags)

Table7.4 Lag Length selection

VAR Lag Order Selection Criteria
Endogenous variables: LNINF
Exogenous variables: LNEXC LNFDI LNGDP LNGE LNMS LNTB LNTOB LNTX LNUMP
Date: 01/12/19 Time: 17:07
Sample: 1981Q1 1992Q4
Included observations: 43

Lag	LogL	LR	FPE	AIC	SC	HQ
0	30.13788	NA	0.022043	-0.983157	-0.614534	-0.847221
1	41.06437	16.77089*	0.013925	-1.444854	-1.035273*	-1.293813
2	42.72192	2.467052	0.013546*	-1.475438*	-1.024899	-1.309293*
3	43.28641	0.813919	0.013872	-1.455182	-0.963684	-1.273933
4	43.68733	0.559415	0.014326	-1.427318	-0.894862	-1.230964

* indicates lag order selected by the criterion
LR: sequential modified LR test statistic (each test at 5% level)
FPE: Final prediction error
AIC: Akaike information criterion
SC: Schwarz information criterion
HQ: Hannan-Quinn information criterion

According to the table 7.4 both lag 1 and 2 are selected by lag selection criterion. But AIC selected lag order 2.

Then let's calculate the ARDL model.

Eviews Steps : Quick > Estimate Equation > Type dependable variable first and then the independent variables (Here we take inflation rate as the dependent variable because we want to identify the impact of other variables on inflation rate) > Method : Select ARDL from the dropdown list below> Max lag: select 2

Table 7.5 : ARDL(1,1,2,2,2,1,0,1,2,2) Model

Dependent Variable: LNINF
Method: ARDL
Date: 01/19/19   Time: 19:41
Sample (adjusted): 1981Q3 1992Q4
Included observations: 43 after adjustments
Maximum dependent lags: 2 (Automatic selection)
Model selection method: Akaike info criterion (AIC)
Dynamic regressors (2 lags, automatic): LNEXC LNFDI LNGDP LNGE
    LNMS LNTB LNTOB LNTX LNUMP
Fixed regressors: C
Number of models evalulated: 39366
Selected Model: ARDL(1, 1, 2, 2, 2, 1, 0, 1, 2, 2)

Variable	Coefficient	Std. Error	t-Statistic	Prob.*
LNINF(-1)	0.765654	0.193814	3.950458	0.0009
LNEXC	-1.307984	0.635489	-2.058230	0.0536
LNEXC(-1)	1.036906	0.613660	1.689708	0.1074
LNFDI	-0.005291	0.040079	-0.132016	0.8964
LNFDI(-1)	-0.004372	0.054921	-0.079600	0.9374
LNFDI(-2)	0.100905	0.053108	1.899986	0.0727
LNGDP	3.830521	2.884338	1.328042	0.1999
LNGDP(-1)	-12.09143	4.692398	-2.576812	0.0185
LNGDP(-2)	6.805681	3.518245	1.934397	0.0681
LNGE	0.235301	0.709831	0.331489	0.7439
LNGE(-1)	0.413213	0.753673	0.548266	0.5899
LNGE(-2)	-1.195607	0.792276	-1.509079	0.1477
LNMS	-6.948139	2.037012	-3.410947	0.0029
LNMS(-1)	5.252862	2.170192	2.420459	0.0257
LNTB	0.070942	0.157469	0.450514	0.6574
LNTOB	0.060018	0.078163	0.767856	0.4520
LNTOB(-1)	-0.140932	0.091911	-1.533358	0.1417
LNTX	1.172387	0.855397	1.370577	0.1865
LNTX(-1)	-0.267997	0.730577	-0.366830	0.7178
LNTX(-2)	1.126829	0.665581	1.693001	0.1068
LNUMP	-0.814212	0.379841	-2.143562	0.0452
LNUMP(-1)	0.179256	0.424325	0.422449	0.6774
LNUMP(-2)	0.542372	0.310356	1.747579	0.0967
C	33.29034	28.37460	1.173245	0.2552

R-squared	0.958687	Mean dependent var		-2.854737
Adjusted R-squared	0.908676	S.D. dependent var		0.285424
S.E. of regression	0.086255	Akaike info criterion		-1.763508
Sum squared resid	0.141357	Schwarz criterion		-0.780512
Log likelihood	61.91541	Hannan-Quinn criter.		-1.401009
F-statistic	19.16967	Durbin-Watson stat		1.788355
Prob(F-statistic)	0.000000			

*Note: p-values and any subsequent tests do not account for model
    selection.

The model calculation selects ARDL(1,1,2,2,2,1,0,1,2,2) as the best
suited model.

E views Steps : View > Model Selection Summary > Criteria Graph

<u>Identification of Best Suited Model at Different Lag Length</u>

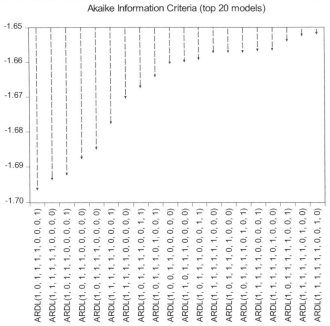

Figure 7.1 AIC Figure for top 20 model of lag length 1

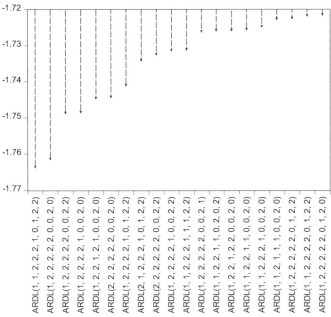

Figure 7.2 AIC Figure for top 20 model of lag length 2

In this study Akaike Information criteria or AIC is used to determine the optimal lag length.. According to the figure 7.1 and 7.2 which displays the AIC value under different applications of lag levels of 1 and 2 , it can be seen that ARDL(1,1,2,2,2,1,0,1,2,2) is the best model for representing the long run relationship between inflation and other selected variables (This ARDL model has the highest negative AIC value, therefore it has the best AIC value).

ARDL Bound test is implemented next to identify if there is long term co-integration exists among the variables under the null hypothesis of "no long run relationship among the variable exists".

Eviews command : view > coefficient diagnostic > long run form and bound test

Table 7.6 Bound Test

F-Bounds Test		Null Hypothesis: No levels relationship		
Test Statistic	Value	Signif.	I(0)	I(1)
		Asymptotic n=1000		
F-statistic	1.083420	10%	1.88	2.99
k	9	5%	2.14	3.3
		2.5%	2.37	3.6
		1%	2.65	3.97
Actual Sample Size	43	Finite Sample: n=45		
		10%	-1	-1
		5%	-1	-1
		1%	-1	-1
		Finite Sample: n=40		
		10%	-1	-1
		5%	-1	-1
		1%	-1	-1
t-Bounds Test		Null Hypothesis: No levels relationship		
Test Statistic	Value	Signif.	I(0)	I(1)
t-statistic	-1.209129	10%	-2.57	-4.56
		5%	-2.86	-4.88
		2.5%	-3.13	-5.18
		1%	-3.43	-5.54

1.08 < 2.14 , 2.14 is the lower critical value at 5% of significance level.

According to the bound test results in table 7.6 F-statistics is 1.08 which is significant at 5% of significance level for finite sample size. Therefore the null hypothesis of no long-run relationship among variables gets rejected. It shows that there is a long run relationship among variables. Therefore an Error correction model should be identified.

Eviews command : View > coefficient diagnostic > error correction form

Table 7.7: Error Correction Model for ARDL(1,1,2,2,2,1,0,1,2,2)

ARDL Error Correction Regression
Dependent Variable: D(LNINF)
Selected Model: ARDL(1, 1, 2, 2, 2, 1, 0, 1, 2, 2)
Case 3: Unrestricted Constant and No Trend
Date: 01/19/19   Time: 20:21
Sample: 1981Q1 1992Q4
Included observations: 43

ECM Regression
Case 3: Unrestricted Constant and No Trend

Variable	Coefficient	Std. Error	t-Statistic	Prob.
C	33.29034	8.313072	4.004578	0.0008
D(LNEXC)	-1.307984	0.381249	-3.430788	0.0028
D(LNFDI)	-0.005291	0.026028	-0.203289	0.8411
D(LNFDI(-1))	-0.100905	0.026741	-3.773387	0.0013
D(LNGDP)	3.830521	1.752654	2.185554	0.0416
D(LNGDP(-1))	-6.805681	2.194108	-3.101799	0.0059
D(LNGE)	0.235301	0.420903	0.559039	0.5827
D(LNGE(-1))	1.195607	0.399677	2.991435	0.0075
D(LNMS)	-6.948139	1.205177	-5.765243	0.0000
D(LNTOB)	0.060018	0.048180	1.245690	0.2280
D(LNTX)	1.172387	0.470900	2.489673	0.0222
D(LNTX(-1))	-1.126829	0.476758	-2.363526	0.0289
D(LNUMP)	-0.814212	0.190070	-4.283739	0.0004
D(LNUMP(-1))	-0.542372	0.184204	-2.944409	0.0083
CointEq(-1)*	-0.234346	0.058648	-3.995772	0.0008

R-squared	0.801745	Mean dependent var	-0.012259
Adjusted R-squared	0.702617	S.D. dependent var	0.130293
S.E. of regression	0.071053	Akaike info criterion	-2.182112
Sum squared resid	0.141357	Schwarz criterion	-1.567740
Log likelihood	61.91541	Hannan-Quinn criter.	-1.955551
F-statistic	8.088004	Durbin-Watson stat	1.788355
Prob(F-statistic)	0.000002		

* p-value incompatible with t-Bounds distribution.

Null hypothesis used to test the significance of parameter as below. Null hypothesis shows that the parameter is zero or parameter is not impacting the model. This null hypothesis should be rejected for a parameter to be significant.

$H_0 : b_i = 0$

$H_1 : b_i \neq 0$

We can find non-significant variables in a created model. Table 7.7 shows the Error Correction Term for ARDL(1,1,2,2,2,1,0,1,2,2). ARDL(1,1,2,2,2,1,0,1,2,2) Model is a over parameterized model. Over parameterized model shows many insignificant co-efficients due to multicollinearity of the regressors. Redundancy test can be applied to make it a parsimonious model by removing most insignificant variables. Notice that in table 7.8 we have checked more variables than highlighted in table 7.7. First apply the insignificant variables into redundant variable test, then in the output model it can be seen that there are more insignificant variables. Redo the redundancy test using those variables as well, after trying many models , select the one which gives out the best outputs. Sometimes according to the eviews version, the output may differs.

Eviews > View > coefficient diagnostics> Error Correction Form

Table 7.8 : Redundant Variable Test

Redundant Variables Test
Null hypothesis: LNFDI LNFDI(-1) LNGE LNGE(-1) LNTX(-1) LNUMP(-1)
Equation: UNTITLED
Specification: LNINF LNINF(-1) LNEXC LNEXC(-1) LNFDI LNFDI(-1)
    LNFDI(-2) LNGDP LNGDP(-1) LNGDP(-2) LNGE LNGE(-1) LNGE(-2)
    LNMS LNMS(-1) LNTB LNTOB LNTOB(-1) LNTX LNTX(-1) LNTX(-2)
    LNUMP LNUMP(-1) LNUMP(-2) C
Redundant Variables: LNFDI LNFDI(-1) LNGE LNGE(-1) LNTX(-1)
    LNUMP(-1) are jointly insignificant

	Value	df	Probability
F-statistic	0.118068	(6, 19)	0.9930

F-test summary:

	Sum of Sq.	df	Mean Squares
Test SSR	0.005270	6	0.000878
Restricted SSR	0.146628	25	0.005865
Unrestricted SSR	0.141357	19	0.007440

Null hypothesis indicate that LNFDI, LNFDI(-1) , LNGE, LNGE(-1), LNTX(-1) and LNUMP(-1) are jointly insignificant.

LNFDI, LNFDI(-1) , LNGE, LNGE(-1), LNTX(-1) and LNUMP(-1) can be identified as the of most insignificant coefficients. Table 7.8 redundant variable test shows that these six variables are jointly insignificant at 5% of significance level.

Table 7.9 Parsimonious Model

Restricted Test Equation:
Dependent Variable: LNINF
Method: Least Squares
Date: 01/19/19   Time: 20:39
Sample: 1981Q3 1992Q4
Included observations: 43

Variable	Coefficient	Std. Error	t-Statistic	Prob.
LNINF(-1)	0.797320	0.120865	6.596761	0.0000
LNEXC	-1.347809	0.501629	-2.686864	0.0126
LNEXC(-1)	0.949064	0.466088	2.036232	0.0525
LNFDI(-2)	0.092907	0.029912	3.105991	0.0047
LNGDP	4.566428	2.219943	2.057003	0.0503
LNGDP(-1)	-12.48260	3.812032	-3.274526	0.0031
LNGDP(-2)	6.493609	2.770739	2.343638	0.0273
LNGE(-2)	-1.247160	0.603317	-2.067173	0.0492
LNMS	-7.330420	1.751360	-4.185558	0.0003
LNMS(-1)	5.549117	1.844421	3.008596	0.0059
LNTB	0.012796	0.123564	0.103560	0.9183
LNTOB	0.060344	0.065799	0.917090	0.3679
LNTOB(-1)	-0.173971	0.063594	-2.735674	0.0113
LNTX	1.162823	0.577296	2.014260	0.0549
LNTX(-2)	1.237544	0.567240	2.181694	0.0387
LNUMP	-0.882883	0.280471	-3.147854	0.0042
LNUMP(-2)	0.594734	0.244298	2.434465	0.0224
C	38.49168	16.13246	2.385976	0.0249

R-squared	0.957147	Mean dependent var	-2.854737
Adjusted R-squared	0.928006	S.D. dependent var	0.285424
S.E. of regression	0.076584	Akaike info criterion	-2.005971
Sum squared resid	0.146628	Schwarz criterion	-1.268724
Log likelihood	61.12838	Hannan-Quinn criter.	-1.734097
F-statistic	32.84609	Durbin-Watson stat	1.809891
Prob(F-statistic)	0.000000		

Table 7.9 parsimonious model is with R square value of 95.71 which means 95.71% of observed values are described by the model. F statistics of the model is significant which proves the model is good and significant. Durbin Watson test statistic is close to 2 which indicate no autocorrelation up to one lag of residuals. The order of the ARDL model is ARDL (p, q_1 , q_2, q_3, q_4, q_5, q_6, q_7, q_8, q_9) / ARDL(1,1,2,2,2,1,0,1,2,2), see that these lag orders have influence on the model (Table 7.9 , lag orders).

After taking this model we should then conduct residual test to validate the model.

Sample: 1981Q1 1992Q4
Included observations: 43

Autocorrelation	Partial Correlation		AC	PAC	Q-Stat	Prob*
		1	0.068	0.068	0.2161	0.642
		2	-0.055	-0.060	0.3595	0.835
		3	-0.107	-0.100	0.9156	0.822
		4	0.211	0.226	3.1282	0.537
		5	-0.174	-0.235	4.6689	0.458
		6	-0.058	-0.003	4.8435	0.564
		7	-0.009	0.031	4.8481	0.678
		8	0.064	-0.048	5.0721	0.750
		9	0.078	0.183	5.4151	0.797
		10	0.195	0.164	7.6508	0.663
		11	0.016	-0.043	7.6659	0.743
		12	-0.124	-0.086	8.6251	0.735
		13	-0.074	-0.064	8.9822	0.774
		14	-0.066	-0.136	9.2769	0.813
		15	-0.245	-0.215	13.438	0.568
		16	-0.163	-0.096	15.352	0.499
		17	-0.042	-0.117	15.483	0.561
		18	0.012	-0.071	15.494	0.628
		19	-0.055	-0.060	15.735	0.675
		20	-0.005	-0.097	15.737	0.733

*Probabilities may not be valid for this equation specification.

Figure 7.3 Diagnostic Tests for ARDL(1,1,2,2,2,1,0,1,2,2)

Eviews command : view > residual diagnostic > Histogram -Normality

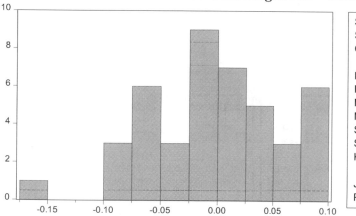

Series: Residuals
Sample 1981Q3 1992Q4
Observations 43

Mean	-2.54e-14
Median	-0.005189
Maximum	0.094226
Minimum	-0.150013
Std. Dev.	0.058014
Skewness	-0.192712
Kurtosis	2.645670
Jarque-Bera	0.491098
Probability	0.782275

Figure 7.4 Normality Test for ARDL(1,1,2,2,2,1,0,1,2,2)

Figure 7.3 the correlogram of squared residuals under null hypothesis residuals are random shows insignificant statistics which confirms the randomness of the residuals. (Null hypothesis : No autocorrelation up to h lags)

Jarque Bera test statistic (Figure 7.4) under null hypothesis the residuals are normally distributed confirms the normality of the residuals.

Eviews command : view > residual diagnostic > Serial Correlation LM

Table 7.10 Breusch Godfrey Test for ARDL(1,1,2,2,2,1,0,1,2,2)

Breusch-Godfrey Serial Correlation LM Test:
Null hypothesis: No serial correlation at up to 2 lags

F-statistic	1.327845	Prob. F(2,17)	0.2912
Obs*R-squared	5.809752	Prob. Chi-Square(2)	0.0548

According to table 7.10 there is no serial correlation up to 2 lags. Here we use 2 lags to test serial correlation because the lag length criteria selected 2 as the best lag.

Eviews command : view > residual diagnostic > Heteroskedasticity Breusch Pagan

Table 7.11 Heteroskedasticity Test for ARDL(1,1,2,2,2,1,0,1,2,2)

Heteroskedasticity Test: Breusch-Pagan-Godfrey
Null hypothesis: Homoskedasticity

F-statistic	0.952571	Prob. F(23,19)	0.5492
Obs*R-squared	23.02891	Prob. Chi-Square(23)	0.4591
Scaled explained SS	3.699614	Prob. Chi-Square(23)	1.0000

There's no heteroskedasticity according to table 7.11. therefore there is no ARCH effect.

Eviews command : view > stability diagnostic > Recursive Estimation
CUSUM test

Figure7.5 CUSUM Test

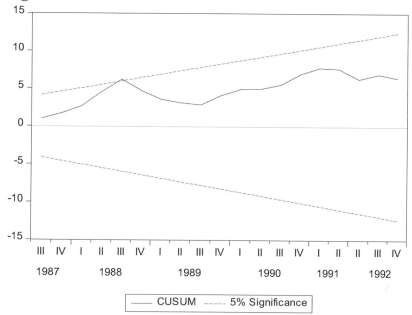

Figure 7.5, CUSUM Test shows that the model is stable at 5% of significance level.

CUSUM test and CUSUSM Square test confirms that the ARDL model is stable at 5% significance level. The time series should between the limit lines for it to be significant.

Eviews command : view > stability diagnostic > Recursive Estimation
CUSUM Square test

Figure 7.6 CUSUM Square Test

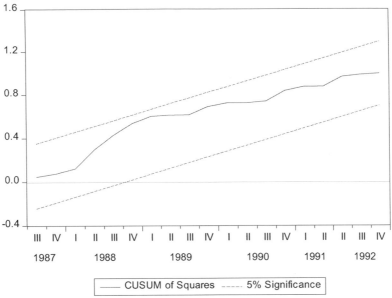

Eviews command : Select Forecast > OK

This command is available in eviews new versions (eviews10/11)

Figure 7.7 : Validation of Model ARDL(1,1,2,2,2,1,0,1,2,2)

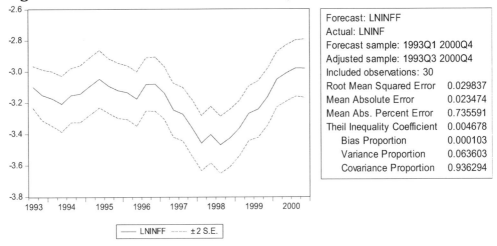

ARDL(1,1,2,2,2,1,0,1,2,2) model which was calculated to model the inflation rate during 1981 Q1 TO 1992 Q4 is predicting the move of the inflation rate during 1993 Q1to 2000 Q4 is as illustrated in figure 7.7.

181

Percentage Error

$$\text{Percentage error} = \left(\frac{(\text{observed value} - \text{predicted value})}{\text{observed value}} * 100 \right)$$

Table 7.13: % Error Table for ARDL(1,1,2,2,2,1,0,1,2,2)

Quarter	LNINFF	LNINF	%Error
1993Q3	-3.09825	-3.13041	-1.02734
1993Q4	-3.15208	-3.13499	-0.54514
1994Q1	-3.17394	-3.18447	-0.33076
1994Q2	-3.20725	-3.21888	-0.36128
1994Q3	-3.15213	-3.10109	-1.64565
1994Q4	-3.14278	-3.15356	-0.34158
1995Q1	-3.09363	-3.11002	-0.52691
1995Q2	-3.04757	-3.05548	-0.25908
1995Q3	-3.09251	-3.1559	-2.00871
1995Q4	-3.12166	-3.15356	-1.01133
1996Q1	-3.13474	-3.1327	-0.06512
1996Q2	-3.1755	-3.10778	-2.17885
1996Q3	-3.0819	-3.08785	-0.1925
1996Q4	-3.07998	-3.03447	-1.49973
1997Q1	-3.13739	-3.08785	-1.60452
1997Q2	-3.24777	-3.22893	-0.58351
1997Q3	-3.2738	-3.26492	-0.27204
1997Q4	-3.36126	-3.35527	-0.17853
1998Q1	-3.45821	-3.48024	-0.633
1998Q2	-3.40353	-3.43579	-0.93897
1998Q3	-3.46953	-3.43579	-0.98202
1998Q4	-3.42605	-3.45144	-0.73552
1999Q1	-3.36222	-3.41428	-1.52474
1999Q2	-3.26866	-3.28876	-0.61111
1999Q3	-3.24174	-3.22893	-0.39679
1999Q4	-3.16225	-3.16061	-0.05195
2000Q1	-3.05018	-3.02413	-0.86121
2000Q2	-3.01153	-3.00578	-0.19107
2000Q3	-2.9801	-2.97007	-0.33791
2000Q4	-2.98068	-2.98578	-0.17081

Percentage error is calculated to identify the validity of the model by comparing the forecasted valued with real observations. ARDL(1,1,2,2,2,1,0,1,2,2) will be compared with the observations of first democratic era which is during 1993 to 2000. Forecasted data lies between percentage error of $\pm$ 10 which is the recommended standard. Model is good for forecasting. LNINFF is estimated values and LNINF is observed values.

This book has covered basic and intermediate level of time series models. There are more types of time series models used in data analysis. But it is necessary to have a good knowledge on the models described in this book to proceed for further complicated models.

Find the data sets for given examples in excel sheet at
https://www.facebook.com/groups/590090104970492/files or
my website http://www.anushabooks.com/product/introduction-to-time-series-analysis/

Visit http://www.anushabooks.com/research/ to read my research works.
For free reading materials use the link
http://www.anushabooks.com/blog/

"Your feedbacks and reviews are encouraging me. Therefore consider leaving a review at amazon.com"

Wish you success in Time Series Data Analysis

Made in the USA
Columbia, SC
06 June 2022

61411560R00104